Welcome to *Getting to Know Our Awesome God*

This 10-session course is designed to
- help students explore who God is and how knowing Him can affect their lives.

During this course students will discover or review:
- what it means to have God as our Father
- the benefits of living in God's will
- ways God provides for His children
- how it is possible to be forgiven and forgive
- ways to respond to temptations
- that God's children can always count on Him
- that God will hold all people accountable for the way they lived on earth
- that God is jealous for the devotion of His people
- the awesome greatness of God.

About Involvement Learning

So often we hear or read accounts of youth who live empty lives and have no apparent goals in life. To fill the emptiness, they often turn to activities that ultimately only heighten that emptiness. Now more than ever, today's youth need to know that the potential to live this dynamic kind of life is firmly rooted in study of and obedience to God's Word.

It takes courage to live an obedient life and it takes strength to overcome the many barriers to Christian growth erected by the world. Therefore, it may not be enough to simply TELL today's youth that studying and obeying God's Word will lead to a productive life. Many teachers have helped their youth KNOW this truth for themselves through involvement learning.

Involvement Learning

The teaching methods and materials in this book emphasize involvement learning. These methods will involve your students in the learning process and take them from the role of passively listening to one of actively digging into the Scriptures. These methods will help you create in your students the desire to examine God's Word and to make practical applications of the truths being studied.

Each session in this Teacher's Manual includes three activities:

- **Approach to the Word**—involves students in activities that capture and direct their interest toward the theme of the session.
- **Bible Exploration**—students use a variety of methods to learn what the Bible says about the session's theme.
- **Conclusion and Decision**—involves each student in a discussion or activity that helps to determine a way to apply the Bible truth to his or her own life.

To give you more flexibility, we include an alternative for each of the three activities. That way, you can choose the activities that best fit the learning styles of your students.

The ideas provided in these sessions may even stimulate additional ideas of your own which fit your group and teaching style. It is our prayer that the learning experiences suggested in this book, coupled with the power of God's Word, will challenge and motivate your students—encouraging some to become Christians and maybe even stirring up those who have grown complacent in their spiritual lives.

Making Flexible Use of *Getting to Know Our Awesome God*

You can use *Getting to Know Our Awesome God* for a summer program, camp or retreat—or for your midweek program ANY time of the year! *Getting to Know Our Awesome God* is designed to be a flexible course—a tool for you to use in the way that best meets your church's needs.

Many youth programs are mere variations of a Sunday morning class or worship experience. It might be necessary for you, the youth leader, to rethink program objectives and to adapt methods and schedule in order to best accomplish your objectives.

If you are responsible for youth, you face programming for one of the most challenging tasks in ministry. There are vast differences in size and maturity from 7th grade to 12th grade (and even more if your group involves 6th graders), between boys and girls, and even within the same grade. The maturity gaps coupled with your students' limitless energy, limited attention span and often unpredictable behavior, make developing a meaningful time of Bible study and fellowship difficult. Not impossible—just difficult!

Older teens are generally more stable, somewhat more interested in serious matters, usually more responsible—but still in need of many similar activities. Use the helpful hints below when you struggle with when to "follow the book" and when to "do your own thing." These hints have worked with other youth groups. Consider how they may be effective with the students you have.

Recreation

Although the central purpose of most meetings is Bible study, some sort of recreational program can very effectively dovetail into the spiritual emphasis. Recreation makes very good sense, because teenagers are very physical and energetic. That energy has to be spent or it will erupt somewhere—usually during a time when you want attention directed at serious business. But recreation also has serious benefits in building relationships, helping newcomers feel a part of the group, helping leaders earn rapport with students, and providing opportunities to put Christian values into real action.

A few tips to keep in mind:

1. Plan your games and acquire your materials in advance. Be at the game site before your students. This will give maximum game time and show that you are in control of the situation, not overwhelmed by it.
2. Use games that will include all of your students. Baseball is fine if you have a bunch of rugged players, or non-involved types who don't mind standing around in the outfield. "Balloon Volleyball" is better to get everyone involved. (See "Games," p. 49.) Other sports can be similarly adapted to make them totally involving.

   Since competition can get out of hand, use wisdom in the competitive nature of the games you play. If one team is getting stomped it is better to bring the game to a close and to re-organize teams. (Don't be afraid to select teams yourself in advance.) Also there are some games and competitions where *every* team can win—not by beating another team but by performing tasks and reaching goals that have a point value given to them. (E.g., points for enthusiasm, good sportsmanship, exhibiting a quality of the fruit of the Spirit, etc.)
3. Don't participate in the games yourself if you have a tendency to "get into it." The kids need objective players, not another big kid.
4. Rugged games played indoors can be loads of fun but make sure you have cleared out any breakable items. Remember—if something can get broken, it will.
5. Have a stock of equipment (balls, markers, whistles, etc.). Make sure the gear is put away to avoid distractions when serious study is attempted. Don't depend on the kids to bring equipment. If it can be forgotten, it will be.
6. It is a good idea to have a well-stocked first aid kit nearby. Kids can find amazingly docile things to scrape and gouge themselves upon. If it seems safe—someone will get hurt.
7. Note that the size and age of your students may cause some unfair advantages during rough play or races. You can offset some of these by having teams compete with equivalent numbers of sizable players or playing the kids in two strings (big and little).
8. It is usually advisable to have recreation before a time of serious study. But some have found it more motivating to have recreation time after a Bible study. You may wish to experiment both ways and see what works best for your group and schedule.

Crowdbreakers, Skits, Etc.

Some groups use devices to get attention and build participation with quick events called crowdbreakers. These often consist of a practical joke or silly game played with a few people while the other kids watch. Naturally most teenagers love to see other kids being made to look foolish (or actually making a fool of themselves). Keep in mind that there are certain kids who will not work well as the recipient of a good-natured joke or as the participant in a silly game. It is best to ask for volunteers for these kinds of events.

Indoor Games

There are vast numbers of indoor games that require very little movement but which a smaller group can find fun and entertaining. Keep in mind to have all your materials prepared in advance and to anticipate rowdiness that might be sparked as a result of an indoor game. (See page 49 for game ideas.)

Fellowship

Teenagers can be very clannish, excluding those who are not part of the "in crowd." Often this is mainly due to shyness, even though it can appear to be snobbishness. Young people often need help from adults to establish friendly contacts with newcomers or regulars who seem a little odd. Try these approaches:

1. Mix outsiders and insiders in recreation activities. Being on a team together can help break a lot of ice.
2. Assign tasks to get specific students to work together.
3. Make a point to introduce kids to each other. Ask a regular to introduce a newcomer to other kids.
4. Talk privately with two or more regulars about ways to include a loner. Avoid saddling one student with someone who is considered unpopular. A teenager often fears that if he or she befriends an outsider, that person will never let go. Having a friend or two share the process is much less threatening.

Singing/Worship

Don't be afraid to dismantle "sacred cows." Sometimes a person may feel compelled to keep something as part of a program just because it is what he or she is used to or it is what the "experts" suggest. For instance, many youth groups feel the need to sing together. But often, only a handful of the kids are singing, a few are faking it and the rest are goofing around or rocking back on their chairs. In this case, re-examine the method used to motivate the kids to sing, take a hard look at the songs (singing the same 14 songs every week will wear thin sooner or later) or even drop singing and substitute something that has more universal participation, such as small group problem solving, role-playing, brainstorming of ideas, conversational prayer, etc. (Singing can always be reinstated at a later time.) Do what works best with your kids to involve them in a meaningful time with God. (See worship ideas on page 6.)

Bible Study

Contrary to popular opinion, teenagers can get serious about God and His Word. But we must use wisdom and common sense as we develop plans to get our students involved in meaningful consideration of God's truths.

It is important in planning the learning part of any youth program to take into consideration the way kids learn best. Teenagers have limited attention spans. They were created to wiggle after sitting no more than 10 minutes (15 on a good day). The success of reaching your students in a meaningful study of the Scriptures depends largely on the "hands on" activities that students are able to do. Kids learn and remember better when they are able to be involved in discovering and applying what God's Word has to say.

Use the most creative means you can devise to stimulate interest in the subject, guide your students into the Scriptures and monitor what your students are discovering. (The variety of ideas in this manual's lesson plans should give you plenty of ideas to keep boredom from taking over your group.)

Teaching

1. Make sure you review each lesson and complete the student activities in advance of each meeting.
2. Be in your classroom ahead of your students, and be the last one to leave.
3. Make sure the room is clean. Try to create an atmosphere that is conducive to study by eliminating distractions and providing the proper ventilation and lighting.
4. Have a good leader-to-student ratio. We suggest a 1-8 ratio in order to build significant relationships and for smooth operation of small group activities. If you do not presently have the staff to maintain this ratio, consider enlisting one or more people to assist you by working under your direction with a small group of students.
5. Make sure you display or give the students an opportunity to share what they have created or worked on.
6. Be in control of the class. Have a few simple, logical rules and state them positively in advance. (E.g., focus on the person who is speaking; only one person speaks at a time; ask a question when you're confused or bored, etc.) Always be sure to have an adult in the control position (the visual focal point) of the class, otherwise the students will take the leadership.

How to Use This Course

Nobody knows your students as you do. No one has the grasp of their interest level, needs, maturity, and spiritual awareness that you have as their leader. Because of this you need to be able to create lessons that meet the real needs of your students. These Bible study materials are designed to help you do just that.

The course book consists of three parts: the **Teacher's Manual Section,** which gives you directions for ten Bible study sessions; the **Student Worksheet Section,** which provides reproducible worksheets; and the **Design-It-Yourself Section** which contains other materials for use with your group both in class and out. Let's take a closer look at these tools and how they may be used.

Teacher's Manual Section:

Each session plan contains the **Key Verse, Biblical Basis, Focus, Aims, Teacher's Bible Study,** and **Session Teaching Plan.**

The Teacher's Bible Study provides you with the background information you need for presenting the session material.

Each **Session Plan** gives you two options for the:

Approach—to catch students' interest;

Bible Exploration—to examine the Scripture and its meaning for life today; and the

Conclusion and Decision—which guides students in making personal application of the Bible truths of the session.

Student Worksheets

This feature allows you to customize the course. These reproducible pages can be used any way you like. You can use them as is or you can cut them up. The basic intent is to involve your students in searching the Scripture, thinking about it, interpreting it, and applying it to their personal lives. The worksheets can be used two ways:

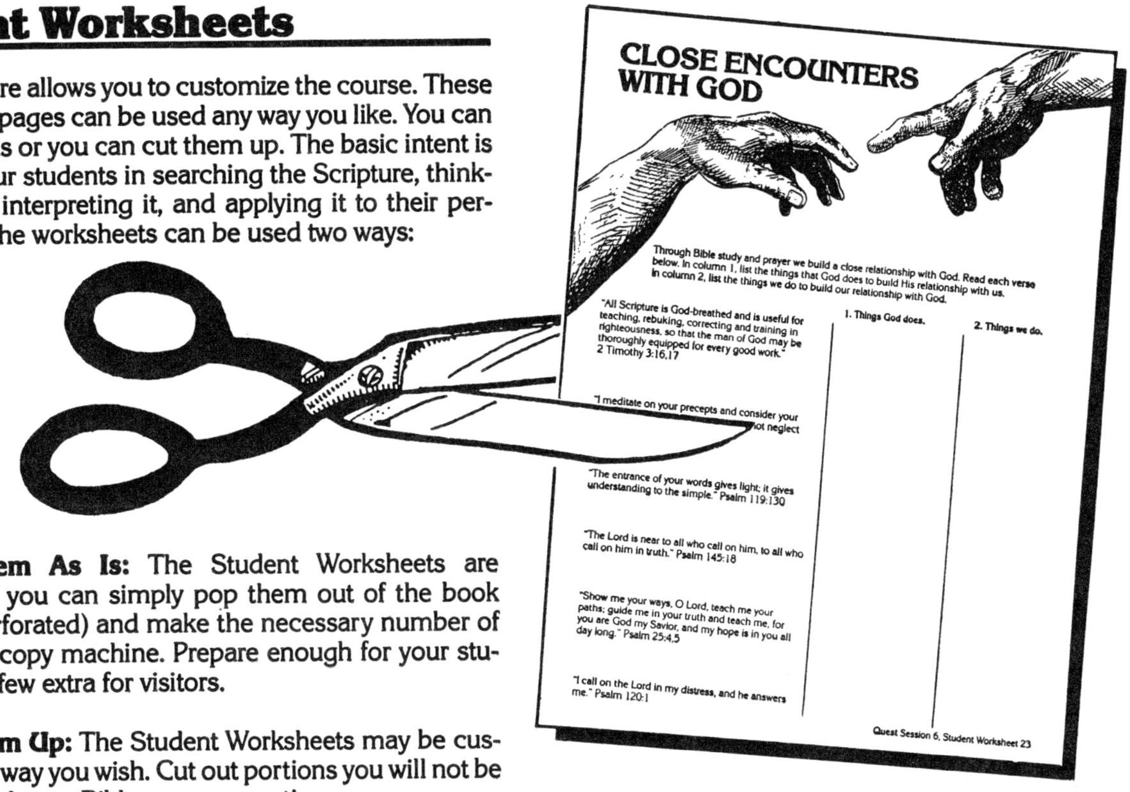
CLOSE ENCOUNTERS WITH GOD

Through Bible study and prayer we build a close relationship with God. Read each verse below. In column 1, list the things that God does to build His relationship with us. In column 2, list the things we do to build our relationship with God.

	1. Things God does.	2. Things we do.
"All Scripture is God-breathed and is useful for teaching, rebuking, correcting and training in righteousness, so that the man of God may be thoroughly equipped for every good work." 2 Timothy 3:16,17		
"I meditate on your precepts and consider your ... not neglect		
"The entrance of your words gives light; it gives understanding to the simple." Psalm 119:130		
"The Lord is near to all who call on him, to all who call on him in truth." Psalm 145:18		
"Show me your ways, O Lord, teach me your paths; guide me in your truth and teach me, for you are God my Savior, and my hope is in you all day long." Psalm 25:4,5		
"I call on the Lord in my distress, and he answers me." Psalm 120:1		

Quest Session 6, Student Worksheet 23

● **Use Them As Is:** The Student Worksheets are designed so you can simply pop them out of the book (they are perforated) and make the necessary number of copies on a copy machine. Prepare enough for your students and a few extra for visitors.

● **Cut Them Up:** The Student Worksheets may be customized any way you wish. Cut out portions you will not be using; add relevant Bible verses, questions, or announcements. Note that the pages are printed on one side only to allow for this. The material is copyrighted, but permission is given for you to use and copy the worksheets as you wish. (This does **not** apply to the Teacher's Manual Section.) Be creative! Use the material selectively, zeroing in on what works for your students.

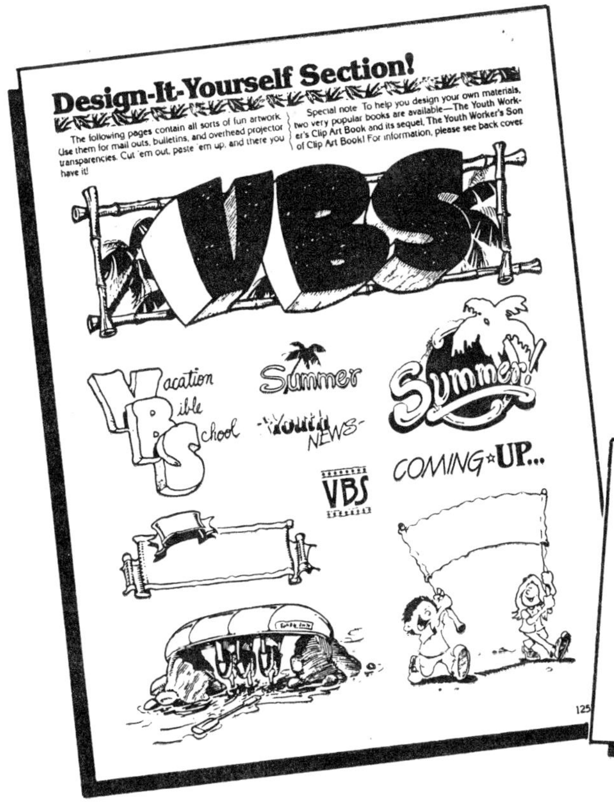

Design-It-Yourself Section:

In this section you will find a number of pages that have absolutely nothing to do with the lessons in the Teacher's Manual Section. These pages are for fun. You may use them to create professional-looking mailers, in church bulletins, or on flyers. Use some of the design elements to create stationery or postcards for your group. Use the cartoons to liven up your Student Worksheets.

Make Something of It: The editors of *Getting to Know Our Awesome God* want the time you spend with your students to be spiritually rewarding. Use the material in this course book to give you ideas, input and guidance—to spark your thinking and creativity. We pray that the tools in this book will help to make your ministry effective for eternity.

Worship

Many youth programs benefit from a lively and dynamic worship time which involves singing, group prayer and motivation. Follow these tips to make your worship times both enjoyable and meaningful.

Singing—Singing has great value for its unique capacity to set a mood and create a sense of participation in community. Many young people who are reluctant to speak up in a group will respond easily to singing. Many who find it difficult to express their thoughts and feelings about God's love in their lives find that songs are an effective vehicle for praise, confession, and even honest doubt.

Singing is frequently used to prepare minds and hearts for the study which will follow. It can be even more effectively used in response to a study just concluded.

Choose your songs carefully, using them not just to fill time, but to purposefully express significant ideas you want your students to remember. Plan for a balance of familiar favorites and a few new songs.

Try one of these creative ideas to enliven your use of songs in worship:

- Have students set the lesson's Key Verse to a familiar tune.
- Have students create a hymn about growing in Christ by writing words to a familiar tune.
- Discuss the meaning of the words of a traditional or Scripture song.

Prayer—Make your prayer time special by establishing a conversational tone. Use everyday language which helps create a bond between people and the Lord. Pray about issues of concern to those in the group, including a balance of thanksgiving and petitions.

To involve your students in prayer, try dividing into groups of about six (too many in the groups intimidate some people, and too few can seem to put individuals on the spot). Encourage students to follow these simple guidelines for prayer in groups:

- Pray for one subject at a time. Wait for at least two or three people to pray for one thing before a new matter is introduced.
- When changing the subject, first affirm what the previous person prayed about.
- Keep prayers brief and conversational. There is no need to try to impress anyone with eloquent oratory.

Motivation—If your worship time precedes the study session, a brief, direct talk can help motivate students to get into the Bible study to come. Raise several issues or questions which the study will address. Or present a recent situation related to the session topic.

If your worship time follows the study, emphasize practical suggestions for applying the truths of that session.

Consider the following creative ideas for involving students in motivating each other:

- Give each student a piece of paper with a Key Verse written on it. Give them three minutes to prepare a 30-second public affairs announcement about their verse and/or its practical application to life. Then ask for several volunteers to read announcements aloud.
- Ask students to talk with a neighbor about the last time someone they know sensed God bringing good out of a difficult or tragic situation. Then invite volunteers to share the example they just heard.
- When talking about becoming more Christlike, lead the group in making a list of people (locally-, nationally- or internationally-known) who represent that quality.

Check How You're Doing

Right after each session do the following:

1. Review the session aims. Did you help students accomplish the aims? What evidence do you have to indicate the goals were reached? If not, why not? What could have been changed? To what degree are you *sure* students understood the main points?
2. Think about your use of time. Were you able to control the time, or did it slip away from you? Did you give students enough warning on time they had to complete their projects? Don't be chained to the clock, but have a timed plan.
3. Consider the appropriateness of the session theme. Were methods and questions right for students? There will be times when you should modify your session plans on the spot to accommodate a question which arises. There are even times when you should put aside the entire lesson and deal with a problem specifically at hand. Unless you thoroughly plan your session, making needed adjustments will be difficult.
4. Think about students' participation. Who talked? Who didn't? Did you ask questions to draw out nontalkers? What questions received immediate answers? Which seemed more difficult? How could you have encouraged more participation?
5. How well are you getting to know your students as individuals? What are their interests, needs and problems? What is their level of spiritual growth? What problems are they having? It takes time and planning to find out this kind of information and you need to stay constantly updated. Plan time to make these conversations happen.

   Take a moment now and list what you know about your students, what you need to know, and what you will do to follow up on their needs.
6. How did the session Scripture affect you as you taught? Were you really involved in the session theme, discussions and activities? Do you think students sensed your enthusiasm and interest? How could you improve?
7. Pray about the past session and the next session. Share fears, joys, failures, and successes with the Lord.

COURSE OVERVIEW

Getting to Know Our Awesome God

Course Focus

This course focuses on knowing God through a study of the Lord's Prayer and attributes of God. As students discover more about who God is, they will be encouraged to respond to Him in practical ways.

Session 1
Our Father
Biblical Basis: Isaiah 9:6; Matthew 6:4,8,9; John 6:32; 14:2,7,23; Romans 8:15; Ephesians 1:5
Focus: God is a loving Father.

Session 2
Your Will Be Done
Biblical Basis: Jeremiah 29:11; Matthew 26:39,42; Luke 15:11-32; John 4:31-34; 5:30; 6:38; Romans 12:2b
Focus: God knows what is best for us, therefore a wise child will follow His voice.

Session 3
Give Us This Day
Biblical Basis: Matthew 6:31-33; 25:35-40; John 21:1-4
Focus: Like a loving father, God listens to our requests and provides for our needs.

Session 4
Forgive Us Our Debts
Biblical Basis: Psalm 103:12; Matthew 6:14,15; 18:21-35; Ephesians 4:32; Hebrews 8:12
Focus: Since our heavenly Father has forgiven us, we must also forgive others.

Session 5
Lead Us Not into Temptation
Biblical Basis: Psalm 119:11; Proverbs 1:10; Matthew 4:1-11; 26:41; 1 Corinthians 10:13; Philippians 4:13
Focus: God can protect us from Satan's temptations as we live in obedience to His Word.

Session 6
Knowing God
Biblical Basis: Psalm 19:8; 25:4; 34:8; 116:1,2; 119:15,16,28,130; 120:1; 145:18; John 10:14; Ephesians 6:18; Philippians 4:6; 2 Timothy 3:16,17
Focus: It is not enough to know about God; He wants us to have a personal relationship with Him.

Session 7
The Faithful God
Biblical Basis: Judges 6-7; Psalm 9:10; 94:14; 121:3,4; Proverbs 2:8; 15:29; 1 Corinthians 1:8,9; Philippians 4:19; 1 John 1:9; 2:25
Focus: We can trust God to be faithful in His care for us.

Session 8
God the Judge
Biblical Basis: Psalm 9:8; Matthew 25; Romans 2:5; 3:22-24; 8:1; 1 Corinthians 3:11-15; Ephesians 2:8-10; Hebrews 4:13; 2 Peter 1:10,11
Focus: God the judge will hold each of us accountable for how we live our lives.

Session 9
The Jealous God
Biblical Basis: Exodus 20:3,4; 34:14; Luke 18:18-23; Romans 8:38,39
Focus: God wants to be number one in the life of each person.

Session 10
The Incomprehensible God
Biblical Basis: Psalm 139:3,4; 145:3; Isaiah 40:12-31; 44:6; 55:8,9; Jeremiah 23:24; John 1:1
Focus: God's greatness is beyond our imagination; He is worthy of our awe and respect.

Things You Will Need for Teaching These Sessions

Be sure to have in your classroom the following supplies and equipment for every session:

- Extra Bibles
- Pens or pencils
- A writing surface and something to write with; for example, chalkboard and chalk, or overhead projector with transparencies and appropriate pens, or large sheets of butcher paper or newsprint with felt pens.
- Individual session plans list the *Student Worksheets* and any special items needed for the particular session.

Our Father

KEY VERSE

After this manner therefore pray ye: Our Father which art in heaven, Hallowed be thy name.
Matthew 6:9 (*KJV*)

BIBLICAL BASIS

Isaiah 9:6; Matthew 6:4,8,9; John 6:32; 14:2,7,23; Romans 8:15; Ephesians 1:5

FOCUS OF THE SESSION

God is a loving father.

AIMS OF THIS SESSION

During this session each learner will:

- EXAMINE attributes of God as our Father;
- DESCRIBE how a person becomes a member of God the Father's family;
- HAVE AN OPPORTUNITY to become a child of God.

TEACHER'S BIBLE STUDY

Adopted by God

All Christians have something in common—God is their Father. The comfort that can be found in this Father-child relationship is expressed in the Scripture passage of Matthew 6:9-13. There we find what is commonly called the Lord's Prayer. But it can also be thought of as the disciples' prayer. For by committing one's life to the loving care of God, thus becoming a disciple, one earns the right to address God as Father.

Jesus said, *You must be born again* (John 3:7). By so stating, He revealed God's desire to adopt as His own child any person who by faith would come to Him through His firstborn Son. In today's lesson, your students will learn what being adopted by God can mean to them.

Teach Us to Pray

It is not recorded in the New Testament that the disciples ever sought instruction about how to perform miracles. They never said, "Wow, Lord, that was neat! Will you show all of us how to walk on water?" However, they did ask Him to teach them how to pray (Luke 11:1). Perhaps they made a connection between all the time Jesus spent alone praying and the mighty works He was able to do.

The Lord's response to the disciples' request was to model the way in which we are to pray. Jesus' prayer lesson is more than a speech to be memorized and recited—rather, it exemplifies the correct spirit and content of prayer. It is the essence of a prayer-life.

Our Father

Jesus began His model prayer with two words. The significance of all that follows in the Lord's Prayer is based on the meaning of those two words—our Father.

In the Old Testament we find examples that speak plainly of Father-God. In Psalm 89:26, the psalmist says, "*You are my Father, my God, the Rock my savior.* The prophet Isaiah proclaimed the name of the Lord to be the Everlasting Father (Isa. 9:6). He also stated, *Yet, O Lord, you are our Father* (Isa. 64:8).

Scripture also contains passages in which God's loving concern is compared to that of a mother (Deut. 32:11,12; Ps. 131; Isa. 66:12,13), providing a balanced portrait of God's deep caring for His children. (Biblical imagery tends to use male designations for God and female designations for Israel or Jerusalem [Old Testament] and the Church [New Testament].)

Although the idea of God as Father was not a new teaching, Jesus' use of "our Father" in the Lord's Prayer shed new light on the concept. Time and again Jesus made reference to God as "my Father" (Matt.

7:21, Luke 22:29, John 6:32, 14:2) and "your Father" (Matt. 6:6,8; Mark 11:25; John 6:37), but by praying "our Father," Jesus is gathering His followers into His intimate relationship with God. This makes it possible for each believer to share a relationship individually with Christ and, at the same time, collectively with one another. By beginning the prayer with the words "our Father," Jesus immediately brings us into the intimate presence of God.

As God's only begotten Son, Jesus alone is able to reveal the Father to the world. What He shows us is every person's ideal parent. All that we can hope for in a father or mother is expressed in Him—He is our protector, He is our provider, He comforts us in our weakness and hurts, He is larger than we are, He wants us to succeed and provides learning experiences for us to grow, He disciplines us in love.

Help your students understand that the Fatherhood of God is not a hope based on fantasy but something they can experience—a real Father's true love. Some of your students may find this hard to accept. They might have concepts of God that are reflections of their earthly fathers who have faults and inadequacies. These students may need help in overcoming a partially negative image of fatherhood. Encourage them to see God as the perfect Father, who loves them far more than a human father could.

Teach your students that by developing and practicing an attitude of "our Father," their prayers will become centered on God first. When time is given at the beginning of prayer to *be still, and know that I am God* (Ps. 46:10), we enter His presence worshipfully, with childlike faith. By focusing on our Father, instead of on our needs and desires, we can effectually quiet our minds to be in tune with Him. This may be difficult for your students to grasp. Some may not see the value in being quiet. Noise has become such a constant part of our world that they may be uncomfortable without it. Impress upon them that it is during these moments of quiet communion that their bond with the Father will be strengthened and they will grow more confident in their relationship with Him.

In Heaven

Being focused on our Father eventually turns our attention above. And by looking up, we will be reminded of how great and powerful He truly is. Addressing Him as our Father "in heaven" helps us to look beyond ourselves and to gaze up at Him in admiration and awe. After coming before God with an attitude of intimacy, the phrase "which art in heaven" reminds us of the majesty and omnipotence of the person we are addressing. God is set above all human experience, able to observe and to intervene in any situation. He is never limited to any place or group, but is Lord of all He surveys. By coming to know Him as the majestic God in heaven, our willingness to recognize His authority will increase.

Hallowed Be Thy Name

The first petition in Jesus' prayer is OUR acknowledgment of HIS holy character and our request to be able to recognize and honor that holiness. When we have established the proper attitude of respect and reverence, God can speak to us. Our minds will be receptive to His voice and we will experience the power of prayer.

Emphasize to your students that we hallow God's name when we pray to Him, when we call upon His name. His name is hallowed when we communicate as children to our heavenly Father.

By learning of their Father's great love and holiness, your students will be encouraged to approach Him in the spirit of adoption which cries out "Abba, Father" (Rom. 8:15).

Notes

APPROACH

Choose one Approach to stimulate your students' thinking about the concept of fatherhood.

APPROACH(5-7 minutes)

Materials needed: Copy for each student of the "What Do You Call Your Parents?" Student Worksheet, pencils.

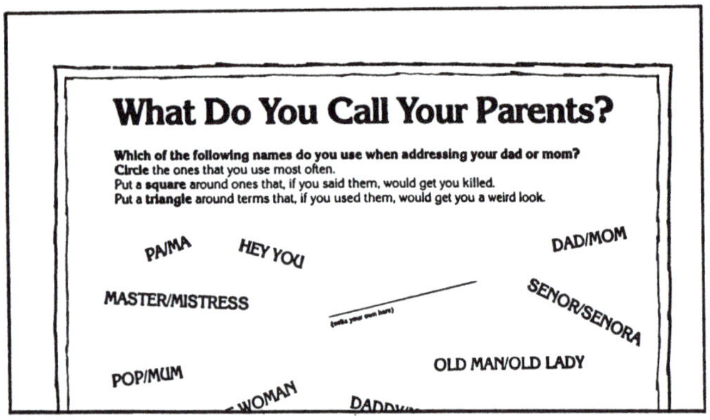
What Do You Call Your Parents?

Which of the following names do you use when addressing your dad or mom?
Circle the ones that you use most often.
Put a **square** around ones that, if you said them, would get you killed.
Put a **triangle** around terms that, if you used them, would get you a weird look.

PA/MA
HEY YOU
DAD/MOM
MASTER/MISTRESS
SENOR/SENORA
OLD MAN/OLD LADY
POP/MUM
WOMAN

Ask your students to complete the "What Do You Call Your Parents?" Student Worksheet. Take a vote of hands to see which terms of address are the least and most common to your group.

Make a transition to the next part of the session by saying something like this: **What word did Jesus use most often when addressing God? He called God "Father" and taught His disciples to do the same. It may surprise some of you to know that another term the followers of Jesus used to describe God was the equivalent of the English word "daddy." What made them able to address God in such a familiar way? Today we will find out.**

ALTERNATE APPROACH(7-10 minutes)

Materials needed: Paper and pencils.

Divide your class into groups of three or four and distribute paper and pencils. Ask each group to work quickly to come up with a list of qualifications (a job description) for the ideal dad or mom. Give them a time limit of five minutes.

When the students have finished, ask several volunteers to share what they have written.

Then make a transition to the next part of the session by saying: **Some of the things you've listed in your job description for a dad are things that are being done for you right now by another Father—a heavenly one. The Bible says God is our Father. Do you think everyone can honestly call God "Father"? Let's look and see what having God as our Father really means.**

EXPLORATION

Use one of the Exploration suggestions to help students learn some attributes of God the Father.

EXPLORATION(45-60 minutes)

Materials needed: Bibles, pencils, drawing paper, shelf or butcher paper, variety of colored felt pens, copy for each student of "The Ideal Father" Student Worksheet.

Preparation: On shelf or butcher paper letter the words to Matthew 6:9-13 (*KJV*). (In this course the *King James Version* will be used for the Lord's Prayer because of its familiarity.) Letter each verse of the Lord's Prayer in a different color. Post chart in a visible location so you can refer to it throughout the course.

Step 1: Ask, **How many of you know the Lord's Prayer?** Recite the prayer together. Instruct students who do not know the prayer to read it from the poster. Say, **Many of us have said this prayer hundreds of times and even know it by heart. But do we really know what it means? One day the disciples asked Jesus to teach them how to pray. He taught them by giving them the Lord's Prayer as an example. The first two words in the prayer are "Our Father." Today we are going to explore what it means that God is our Father and what kind of Father He is.**

Step 2: Pass out pencils and copies of "The Ideal Father" Student Worksheet. Instruct students to draw lines, matching each statement to the verse it describes. Then have each student thoughtfully choose the attribute of God the Father that best meets the most pressing need in his or her life right now. Allow students to share the attributes they chose with the rest of the class.

Step 3: Pass out paper and felt pens. Say, **Today we have discovered what kind of Father God is to His children. He is the ideal Father—taking care of, listening to and enjoying His children. There is something very important you should know though—not everyone is a child of God. Not everyone can call God "Father." In order to call God "Father" you need to become a member of His family. We're going to take a look at how a person**

becomes a member of God's family and receives the right to call God Father. On the chalkboard draw five large boxes. In each box draw a stick figure to illustrate each of the steps to becoming a member of God's family (see illustration). Have students copy your drawings on their own papers as you draw and discuss these points with them:

1. God is Holy. All people are separated from God by sin.
2. God loves us and wants us to be in His family so He sent Jesus to take the punishment for our sins.
3. If we accept Christ as Savior and are willing to live His way, God will forgive our sins.
4. Then God can accept us into His family. Because Jesus took our punishment, we're declared not guilty and He sees us as holy.
5. We begin a whole new life as God's child.

Step 4: Divide class into pairs. Have the members of each pair use their illustrations to explain to each other how to become a member of God's family.

(Note: You may want to use the article, "Introducing Young People to Christ," as a basis for this presentation. Point out that many people believe that attending church or giving to charity or not stealing or doing good works will earn a position as God's child. Stress that only trust in Jesus Christ as Savior and Lord brings forgiveness from sin and new life with Him.)

Summarize by briefly sharing your own experience of accepting Christ—and thus beginning a trusting relationship with God your Father. Emphasize how your relationship with Him has provided one or more of the benefits the group discussed earlier.

ALTERNATE EXPLORATION(60 minutes)

Materials needed: Bibles, paper, scissors, felt pens, an envelope for every three to four students, glue, overhead transparency and projector or newsprint or chalkboard and chalk.

Preparation: Letter the words from the list below on a sheet of paper, leaving space between each letter. (Note: These words are key words from the *New International Version*. If your class uses a standard reference different from the *NIV*, you might want to look up the verses and make up your own list of key words.)

Words: COUNSELOR, FATHER, GOOD, INSTRUCTS, REFUGE, CARES, LOVES, GUIDE.

Cut the paper into squares so that each square contains one letter (see illustration below). Place all the squares in an envelope. Repeat procedure, making one set of letters for every three to four students.

Copy the verse references listed below onto an overhead transparency, newsprint or chalkboard.

Verses: Psalm 25:8;48:14; Isaiah 9:6; Nahum 1:7; John 15:9; 1 Peter 5:7.

Step 1: Ask your students to work in groups of three or four. Distribute a Bible, paper, glue and an envelope full of letters to each group. Post the Bible verse references. Have each group look up the posted verses, find key words describing God and assemble key words from the lettered squares. Tell students they have 12 minutes to complete the activity. (Students glue the letters onto a piece of paper to form words.) When groups have completed the activity, ask them to share the key words they found. Invite volunteers to explain the main thought of each verse. Ask, **Why do you think this verse is important to our understanding of God?**

Step 2: Same as *Step 3* in original Exploration.

Step 3: Same as *Step 4* in original Exploration.

CONCLUSION

Use one of the suggested Conclusion methods to help students describe how a person becomes a member of God's family.

CONCLUSION(5-7 minutes)

Materials needed: Copies of "Kids Wanted" Student Worksheet, pencils.

Ask your students to work individually on the "Kids Wanted" Student Worksheet. After three or four minutes, invite volunteers to share what they have written. Close by inviting any students who want to talk further about having God as their Father to stay behind and do so. End in prayer, thanking God for being a loving Father who cares for all His children.

ALTERNATE CONCLUSION(7-10 minutes)

Materials needed: Construction paper, scissors, ribbon, gold seals, felt pens, glue.

Invite each student to create a personal note to God out of the materials you provide. Explain that their note should state when, why and how they became a child of God. Allow students the opportunity to share what they have created, but do not put anyone on the spot. Encourage each person to keep their note with them and read it as a prayer several times in the next few days.

Close in prayer thanking God for the privilege of being adopted into His family. Invite those who can't honestly say that God is their Father to stay and discuss things with you.

EXTRA FEATURES

Add one or more of these features to your session to increase friendship and impact:

Worship—see page 6.
Games—see page 49.
Munchies—see page 48.
Crafts—see page 50.

Your Will Be Done

KEY VERSE
Thy kingdom come. Thy will be done in earth, as it is in heaven. Matthew 6:10 (*KJV*)

BIBLICAL BASIS
Jeremiah 29:11; Matthew 26:39,42; Luke 15:11-31; John 4:31-34; 5:30; 6:38; Romans 12:2

FOCUS OF THE SESSION
God knows what is best for us, therefore a wise child will follow His voice.

AIMS OF THIS SESSION
During this session each learner will:
- REVIEW the story of the lost son;
- DISCOVER the benefits of living in God's will;
- IDENTIFY areas in his or her life that need to be changed in order to be in God's will.

TEACHER'S BIBLE STUDY

Thy Kingdom Come

The first petition of the Lord's Prayer is that God's name will be hallowed; the second, that His Kingdom will come. The Kingdom of God (or Kingdom of Heaven) is mentioned over 100 times in the Gospels, 49 times in Matthew alone. Yet it is not a physical place. Jesus said it is within you (Luke 17:21). In its broadest sense, God's Kingdom is the sphere of His control. God's kingdom is His power manifest in us and in the world.

By praying "Thy kingdom come" we are making a threefold request. It is first very personal: "I want to live as your child, subject to your authority so that you will be glorified." Second, it is a request that His authority will become increasingly evident on the earth. Third, it is a prayer for the future establishment of His eternal kingdom.

Thy Will Be Done

Today's session will focus on the third petition of the Lord's Prayer: Thy will be done. This petition grows naturally from the first two. God's will is tied very closely to His hallowed name. Anyone who takes on His name through adoption and calls Him Father will want to live in His kingdom and do His Will.

God has given each of us a free will. With our wills we can choose to pursue our own desires and live for ourselves or we can choose to pursue God's desires and live for Him. When we pray, "Thy will be done" we are saying that we have chosen to put aside our own desires for the higher goal of doing God's will and bringing Him glory.

Jesus taught His disciples to pray, "thy will be done." This was also the ruling principle in His own life and prayers. (See Matt. 26:39,42; John 4:34; 5:30.) In John 6:38 Jesus said, *For I have come down from heaven not to do my will but to do the will of him who sent me.* Jesus had made the choice to pursue the goal of doing His Father's will and bringing Him glory. Even in the most difficult situations this principle guided His life, as seen in Matthew 26:39: *My Father, if it is possible, may this cup be taken from me. Yet not as I will, but as you will.*

It need not be a burden to do the will of God but a privilege and a joy. The better we know Him and are in communion with Him, the more our desires will become the same as our God's. Psalm 37:4 illustrates this: *Delight yourself in the Lord and he will give you the desires of your heart.*

My Will Be Done

If we are delighting in something other than the Lord then we probably are not desiring to do His will. We are choosing to live by self-will and in a sense praying, "My will be done."

If we do not purposefully seek to do God's will, our free will becomes self-will. This self-will, or pride, acts like spiritual cataracts clouding our vision. It soon becomes impossible to see clearly. We forget that God alone can see the complete picture of our lives (Isa. 55:8). So when circumstances or feelings don't seem quite right, we grab the reins of our lives. And in the process we lose sight of the fact that God wants to work out through our lives what is best for us, not necessarily what is easiest or the most enjoyable. When this self-will takes over, it is very easy to stumble and fall in our spiritual walk (Prov. 16:18).

A Lost Son's Dilemma

One of Jesus' best known parables, the story of the lost son (Luke 15:11-32), illustrates what happens when self-centeredness blinds a person to what is God's best for him or her.

In the story we find a father who maintains a large estate that can completely meet the needs of all who live there. The man has two sons. The older son is content to stay at home but the younger son wants to leave, so he asks for his inheritance (v.12). His father gives him his share and shortly afterward the son leaves home.

It appears that the problem here is not that the boy wanted to leave. Children grow up and leave home as a natural course of events. The young man's problem seems to be his *reason* for leaving. He wanted to control his own life and desired to spend the money *when* and *how* he saw fit, thinking he knew better than his father did (v.13).

The father's response to his son's selfish request was the same as God's response to us when we pray, "my will be done." He let him go. God never forces or imposes His love on anyone. But He is quick to forgive and welcome us home after we find out that we can't make it alone.

The son's problems began immediately and went from bad to worse. To start with, his request limited his resources. When he was under his father's authority he had everything he needed. When he received what was his, he had only one-third of his father's property (v.12). Remind your students that when we go our own way and "do our own thing" we are in a sense cutting ourselves off from God and His resources.

Jesus' story indicates that it did not take the son long to squander his wealth (v.13). When we are operating on our own and relying on human wisdom we can and do make bad choices which leave us quickly bankrupt—not necessarily financially, but spiritually. But when we are living in God's Kingdom, doing His will, the Father's wisdom and strength are available to sustain us, even in difficult times.

The young man not only ran out of money, but the circumstances surrounding him also turned bad—there was a famine (v.14). Not only was he out of money to buy things, now there wasn't anything to buy or even beg. He couldn't even scrounge the scraps from the pigs he was feeding (v.16). When we are out of God's will, bleak circumstances may present a hopeless picture and we can feel trapped with no way of escape.

The Lost Son Returns

Finally, in total despair, the son remembered and returned to his father. Jesus said, "he came to his senses" (v.17). Stripped of his pride, the son realized he had been wrong. He discovered that following his own will separated him from the love and blessings he had while with his father. He now valued his father and the privileges of being his son, and in humility he returned to his father.

It is not until we come to our senses and return to the Father that we can enjoy any measure of the joy and provision of His love. Should we, as heirs of God, choose to take what is ours and squander it, God the Father will be waiting to welcome us back with forgiveness when we return to Him in repentance. And just like the lost son, we will be overwhelmed by what is in store for us when we return to His kingdom and the authority of His will.

Four Guidelines

There are several guidelines that can help us in knowing and doing God's will. First, we must *desire to do His will.* If we have given our lives to God then we have surrendered our own desires to do the will of God. We can affirm that decision with the daily attitude expressed in Psalm 143:10, *Teach me to do your will, for you are my God; may your good Spirit lead me on level ground.*

Second, we must *look to God's Word to communicate His will.* We cannot rely on outward circumstances, or even feelings to discern what God's will might be. But we can always rely on the guiding principles in His Word. The better we know His Word and apply it to our lives the more confident we can be that we are doing God's will. As we spend time in God's Word we will be motivated to do God's will. Psalm 40:8 says, *I desire to do your will, O my God; your law is within my heart.*

Third, we should *remain in the company of—and seek counsel from— others who are also seeking to please God.* From godly friends we can receive wise counsel as we seek to understand and do God's will.

Fourth, we must *trust God* that as we surrender ourselves to do His will, He will meet our needs.

Be sure to make these four guidelines clear as you and your students discuss God's will during the Bible Exploration. Of all the practical lessons you can teach your students, guidance in seeking and knowing God's will is key. This lesson can provide powerful insights to help your students wisely make the major decisions facing them in the years to come.

Notes

APPROACH

Choose one Approach to direct the students' thinking about obedience to parents.

APPROACH(5-7 minutes)

Materials needed: A pet of some sort in a suitable box or case (cat, goldfish, parakeet, etc.).

Bring the pet to the front of the classroom and gain the group's attention. Then command the animal to do a series of tricks (which of course the animal can't do). Ask the class to tell you why the pet won't cooperate. Ask, **Why do you think my pet didn't obey me?** (Animal is too dumb, doesn't understand English, is too young, isn't trained, etc.) **Why don't people always obey? What are some reasons young people sometimes don't obey their parents?**

Make a transition to the next part of the session by saying something like this: **When our parents ask us to do something, we have a choice to make. Unlike most animals, we CAN follow their advice and instructions. Even though our parents aren't perfect, usually they want what is best for us and if we follow their guidance it will be to our benefit. God, unlike our parents, IS perfect. We can be confident that following His advice (His will) will be what is best for us and for others.**

ALTERNATE APPROACH(5-7 minutes)

Materials needed: Felt pens, large sheet of butcher paper or newsprint, masking tape or tacks.

Before class begins, post the butcher paper on the wall and distribute felt pens so that they are in easy reach of the students. Write this question on the paper: "Why do kids run away from home?" As students enter the class, ask each to write on the paper one plausible answer to the question.

Move to the Exploration by saying something like this: **You have given many reasons why kids may run away from home. Today we are going to take a look at a young man who left home, choosing to live his own way—apparently thinking he knew better than his father.**

EXPLORATION

Use one of the Exploration suggestions to lead students in exploring aspects of the will of God.

EXPLORATION(60 minutes)

Materials needed: Bibles, chalkboard and chalk (or newsprint and felt pen), pencils, copy for each student of the "Junior Come Home!" and "The Shredded Sheet" Student Worksheets, scissors, construction paper, felt pens.

Step 1: Write on chalkboard, "Your will be done." Say, **This request is one of the hardest parts of the Lord's Prayer. Most people want to do "their own thing." Today we're going to see where our own will leads us.** Distribute worksheets and pencils. Ask your students to read the story called "Junior Come Home!" on their student worksheets. Then have them look up Luke 15:11-31 and read the story in their Bibles.

Then ask questions such as: **What do you think was this young man's biggest mistake? Why do you think he wanted his own way instead of following his dad's advice? If you'd been his best friend, what could you have said to talk him out of his hare-brained plan?**

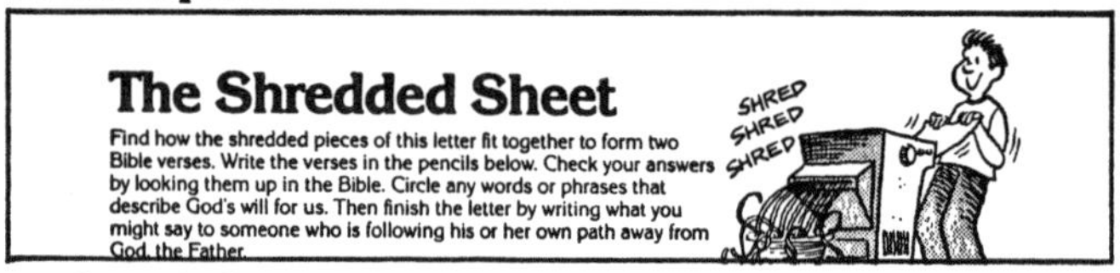

Step 2: Students work individually on the "The Shredded Sheet" worksheet, finding how the torn-up pieces of the letter fit together to form two Bible verses. Students then write the verses and check their accuracy by looking in the Bible. Direct students to circle any words or phrases that describe God's will for us.

Step 3: Regain the attention of the class and ask students to repeat the verses they pieced together. Then have each student write a letter to an imaginary friend who is not following God's will. They can use ideas from the story of the lost son, as well as from the verses they read in *Step 2.* Their letters should try to communicate to their friends the value of doing God's will. After allowing students about 10 minutes to work, encourage them to share the letters they wrote. Ask, **Why are we often not willing to accept good advice? What could we do to help a friend accept the advice we've given?** Add comments from the Teacher's Bible Study to make sure these points are emphasized: (1) We must want to do God's will. (2) We must look to God's Word to communicate His will to us. (3) We should remain in the company of—and seek counsel from—others who are seeking to please God. (4) We must trust God to meet our needs.

Step 4: Distribute scissors, construction paper and felt pens. Students work together to create a bulletin board display (see sketch).

Post the following Bible references in a visible location: Psalm 143:10; Proverbs 3:5; Proverbs 14:12; Jeremiah 29:11; Matthew 6:10; Romans 12:2; 1 John 2:17. Each student chooses one verse to look up and creates a road sign based on that verse. (Note: If you have many students who are unfamiliar with the Bible, be prepared to help them understand the concepts in these verses.) Some verses may have a phrase appropriate for God's Way Road and a phrase for Own Way Avenue. Students may make a sign for each phrase. Students post encouraging signs on God's Way Road and warning signs on Own Way Avenue.

ALTERNATE EXPLORATION(60 minutes)

Materials needed: Copy for each student of the "Take My Advice, Kid," "Junior, Come Home!" and the "The Shredded Sheet" Student Worksheets, pencils, Bibles, "The Lost Son Game" Student Worksheet reproduced on heavy paper (one sheet for every two students), scissors, envelopes.

Preparation: Cut out the cards on "The Lost Son Game" Student Worksheet. Place each set of 30 cards in an envelope. One set will be needed for every two students.

Take My Advice, Kid

In the following blanks write what you think MIGHT happen in each situation . . . (There are no right or wrong answers.)

Step 1: Direct students to complete the "Take My Advice, Kid" worksheet. Be sure to tell the students this is not a test with right or wrong answers, but an idea-generating activity intended to help people start thinking about following advice and instructions. When students have completed worksheet lead them in sharing their responses with the class.

Step 2: Say, **Today we're looking at what "Thy will be done" means. Based on your own knowledge of fathers, see where you think Junior probably didn't follow his dad's will in this story.** Ask students to individually read "Junior, Come Home!" from their worksheets.

THE LOST SON GAME

Cut out the cards below and on the following page. Mix them up and spread them out on a table facedown. Play the game with two or three other people. Take turns turning over two cards at a time, trying to match each situation with the card that describes it. When a match is made, player collects those two cards. The winner is the person with the most

Step 3: Divide class into groups of two or three. Give each group an envelope of 30 cards cut from "The Lost Son Game" Student Worksheet. Instruct each group to mix up cards and spread them out on a table facedown. Group members take turns turning over two cards at a time, attempting to find a situation and illustration that match. When a match is found the player collects the matching cards. When all cards are collected the game is over and the player with the most cards wins.

Conclude by asking these questions: **Why do you think the lost son left home? What do you think the son learned through his experience? When has going your own way ever landed you in trouble?** Briefly share an event from your own life when your willfulness created problems for you and/or others.

Step 4: Same as *Step 2* in original Exploration.

Step 5: Same as *Step 3* in original Exploration.

CONCLUSION

CONCLUSION(5-7 minutes)

Materials needed: Small index cards, pencils.

Distribute an index card and pencil to each student. Remind your students that when we go our own way and "do our own thing" we cut ourselves off from God. We can choose to mess up our lives, just like the lost son did. But we can also choose what is God's will for us—to live as His children.

Have each student draw a vertical line to divide index card in half. Ask each student to write on one half of index card an area in his or her life that may not be in God's will. Then instruct them to write on the other half a way they could change their actions or attitudes in that area to follow God's will. (Inform students that these cards are private. No one else will see them.) Say, **God wants the best for you. That is His will. Each time you pray the Lord's Prayer and say, "Thy will be done," remember that God knows what is best for you. You CAN do His will by trusting in our Father's love and guidance.**

Close in prayer, thanking God for being a forgiving, welcoming Father who will help us to do His will.

ALTERNATE CONCLUSION(10-15 minutes)

Materials needed: Pencils or felt pens, paper.

Brainstorm with students the areas of their lives in which it is difficult to live by God's will. Write students' ideas on chalkboard. (Examples: obeying parents, being honest at school, loving enemies, thinking clean thoughts.) Divide the class into small groups, assigning each group one of the areas listed on the chalkboard. Each group has five minutes to prepare a 30-second skit enacting that situation. The first part of each skit should show the result of not following God's will, the second part should show the result of acting in God's will. Have groups perform their skits.

Close in prayer. Thank God that we can know His will and ask for help in following Him.

EXTRA FEATURES

Add one or more of these features to your session to increase friendship and impact:

Worship—see page 6.
Games—see page 49.
Munchies—see page 48.
Crafts—see page 50.

Give Us This Day

KEY VERSE

Give us this day our daily bread. Matthew 6:11 (*KJV*)

BIBLICAL BASIS

Matthew 6:9-11;31-33; 25:35-40; John 21:1-14

FOCUS OF THE SESSION

Like a loving father, God listens to our requests and provides for our needs.

AIMS OF THIS SESSION

During this session each learner will:

- IDENTIFY from Scripture some ways God provides for us;
- LIST ways he or she can be used to show God's care to others;
- CREATE a prayer that expresses needs, as well as thankfulness for God's giving nature.

TEACHER'S BIBLE STUDY

Breakfast on the Beach

One day following the Lord's resurrection, Peter and the other disciples went fishing. They spent all night in the boat but caught no fish. Early in the morning Jesus appeared on the shore, but the disciples did not recognize Him. He told them to throw their net on the right side of the boat and then they would catch some fish. The disciples did what He said and caught so many fish (153) that they weren't even able to haul the net into the boat. At that point, John knew the Man on the shore was Jesus and he said to Peter, "It is the Lord!". Immediately Peter dove into the water and swam the hundred yards to shore. The others followed in the boat. What did the glorified Lord have waiting for them? Breakfast! Even though Jesus had important business to conduct with Peter, He knew the disciples would be hungry. So He cooked some fish and toasted some bread for them.

Throughout His ministry Jesus concerned Himself with the physical needs of His disciples and the crowds that followed Him. He was (and still is) well aware that a person's outlook and faith are affected by an empty stomach. It is no surprise that Jesus included asking for daily bread in His lesson on prayer.

Our Daily Bread

To fully understand "give us this day our daily bread," it is important to view today's Scripture lesson in the light of our two previous lessons on the Lord's Prayer. We find Matthew 6:11 following Jesus' instructions about a holy, heavenly Father who wants us to obey His will. But He is not some cosmic policeman. The broader context of Jesus' teaching shows us God is our Father who can be approached in prayer.

Because our heavenly Father is a loving, trustworthy, approachable God, He is concerned about our daily, physical needs. Many people spiritualize the passage "Give us this day our daily bread," interpreting it to mean God's Word—spiritual food. And we do need to partake of this food daily in order to grow spiritually. But because God is concerned with our daily, physical needs, it is not unlikely that Jesus was literally referring to our need for bread—or food, in general. The God who designed our bodies is concerned about them and wants us to talk to Him about our physical needs.

God, Our Provider

Through this simple petition to have our everyday needs met, certain tremendous truths emerge.

First, this request once again gives God His proper place in our lives. The Father is our ultimate provider. We are admitting that it is from Him that we receive the food necessary to sustain us. This is similar to an infant crying out to his parents because of hunger or some other physical discomfort. The big difference of course is that we still must carry the responsibility of working for our food. We cannot assume that God will magically "give" us food, but rather, the ability to work and earn our food comes from His hand.

Second, we are taught to live one day at a time. The prayer is for *daily* bread. Fretting about possible future shortages betrays a lack of faith and is a distraction from more valuable commitments. We see this illustrated in Exodus 16 when the children of Israel were given manna each morning. They were instructed to gather only enough for the upcoming day and not to save any for the next day. In this manner they were fed for forty years. We never read of any of them perishing due to hunger.

The Story of George Müller

In more recent times God worked to meet the daily needs of His servant George Müller, in Bristol, England. (This story is told on the "Give Us This Day Our Daily Bread" Student Worksheet.) In 1835 many children in England were homeless and working long hours to support themselves. George Müller was led by God to open an orphanage to ease the pain and suffering of those homeless children. He did it with no money of his own, simply by prayer. Shortly after beginning to pray, and without making any public pleas, provisions began to arrive at Müller's home.

Within several months George Müller had his first orphanage. By the end of the first year there were three, each one a product of George Müller's private prayer. He never asked for public support. He and his staff fed, clothed and housed two thousand orphans. They also raised millions of dollars to pay for this endeavor, much of it not coming until the very instant it was needed.

Müller's concept was that God could and would keep His promises and supply the daily bread of his children.

God Provides Necessities

A third lesson is that God provides what is necessary. We are told to pray for daily bread, not for daily desserts. The fact of the matter is that God does not always give us what we want but does give us all we need. For example, few parents give their children everything that they "desire." A child may desire to spend all of the money received from birthday gifts. The parent may require that a portion of the money be put into a savings account. Even though the child may be protesting loudly, wise parents know that what they are doing is in the best interest of the youngster. With time, the heart's desire of the child changes and the money tucked away in the savings account becomes valued and appreciated. The child may even express gratitude for being made to save. The parent's wisdom is understood.

As we mature as children of God and learn of His will, we grow to rely on the Father's wisdom. And we reduce the danger of asking for the wrong things. We in fact find ourselves asking for the kind of bread God wants us to have. As this begins to happen we start to realize the fulfillment of God's promise to give us the desires of our hearts (Ps. 37:4).

Sharing Our Bread

Finally, we are taught not to be selfish in our prayers. The fact that we are in a world where many lack even the basic necessities of food and covering can only lead us to the conclusion that God desires that we who have an excess share with those who are wanting. In this way we become part of the answer to the prayers of those in need. (After all, Jesus taught us to pray for "our" daily bread, not "my" daily bread.)

We are to look to our Father God in faith and love to supply us with all we really need to enable us to live according to His will. If we are close to the heart of God's Son, Jesus, we will feel His love and compassion. These two aspects of His character will move us to serve others and to pray not only to receive our daily bread but to share it as well. In so doing we minister to the very one who gives to us. He told us Himself that if we feed, clothe, visit or give water to the least of His brothers we do it unto Him (Matt. 25:35-40).

Today's session on the Lord's Prayer illustrates our dependence on God, our trust in God, and challenges us to take and share the gifts of God with others. As we ask for our daily bread we receive much more than we request from the Giver of all good gifts. And He has great joy in giving.

Notes

THIS WEEK'S TEACHING PLAN

APPROACH

Choose an Approach activity to start students thinking about asking and receiving.

APPROACH(5-7 minutes)

Materials needed: Copies for each student of the "How 'Bout a Raise?" Student Worksheet, pencils.

Distribute worksheets and pencils to students. Instruct them to complete the "How 'Bout a Raise?" matching activity.

Have several students share what they have recorded and then move to the Exploration by asking, **What are some things you've asked God for?** Then say something like this: **Today we are going to take a look at one of the most common ways people view God—the giving God. I think we will find out that there is much to be learned about God's giving.**

ALTERNATE APPROACH(5-7 minutes)

Materials needed: Copies for each student of "Give Us This Day Our Daily Bread" Student Worksheet.

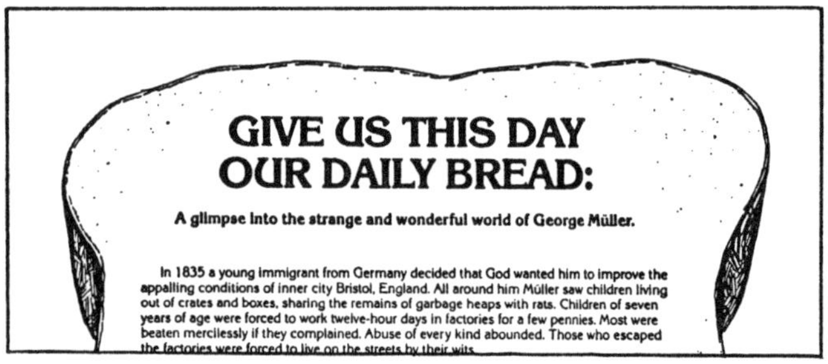

Ask your students to read the story of George Müller on their worksheets. (Or read the story aloud as students follow on their worksheets.) Then ask a few questions such as: **Do you think George Müller was brave or foolish? Why? What does this story tell you about God? What are some examples of how God provides for His children in this way today?**

Make a transition to the Exploration by saying something like this: **Today we are going to take a look at the God who loves to give to His children. We will explore some of the ways God provides for us and some ways we can respond to His care.**

EXPLORATION

Use one of the Explorations to help students discover ways God provides for His children.

EXPLORATION(55-60 minutes)

Materials needed: Bibles, copies for each student of both "No Comment" Student Worksheets, pencils or pens, butcher or shelf paper, felt pens, masking tape.

Step 1: Review the Key Verses for Sessions 1 and 2. Distribute Bibles and ask students to read Matthew 6:11. Ask, **Why do you think Jesus wanted us to ask for daily bread?** (To acknowledge the fact that God is the source of our food; to help us remember to live one day at a time; to remind us that God will provide the necessities, not the luxuries; to make us aware of God's desire for us to provide for those who have less than we do.)

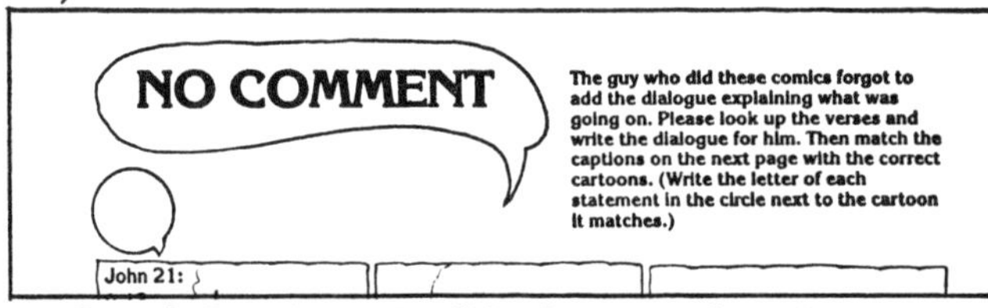

Step 2: Distribute the "No Comment" worksheets and pencils. Students work individually to look up each Scripture passage, write in the dialogue and then match the captions found on page two to the appropriate cartoons. Share comments on each concept using material from the Teacher's Bible Study.

Step 3: Letter the question "How does God meet our needs through . . . ?" on the chalkboard. Help students form three groups. Distribute a sheet of butcher or shelf paper and a felt pen to each group. Direct each group to choose a "scribe" who letters one of the following headings on his or her group's poster—"Family," "Nature" or "Others" (see sketch).

Explain that each group is to brainstorm answers to the question on the chalkboard. For instance, one group will talk about how God provides for their needs through families. Possible answers might include: dad earns money, mom buys groceries, everybody helps cook, mom has a job, grandpa grows a garden—God has given each person the ability to work. The scribe then lists their answers on the group's poster.

When posters are finished, hang them in a visible location. Then have students look up Matthew 25:35-40 in their Bibles.

Ask, **What does this passage from Matthew say about our responsibility to share? One way God provides for people's needs is through other people. In what ways can you help others to have their "daily bread"?** (For example, in nature God has provided the means to grow food—light, water, soil. We can do our part by taking care of the earth, not contributing to water or air pollution, using our resources wisely, etc. In our families we can help by not wasting food, by working to earn money, etc. We can also give food, money, clothing and education to others and give our time to help those who are in need.) As students share ideas, write them on the appropriate poster.

ALTERNATE EXPLORATION(55-60 minutes)

Materials needed: Bibles, paper, pencils or pens, butcher or shelf paper, felt pens, masking tape, chalk and chalkboard.

Preparation: Letter the following references on the chalkboard: Matthew 6:11,25-34; 1 Timothy 6:6-10.

Step 1: Distribute Bibles and have students look up verses. Read verses aloud, asking students to listen and look for any contrasting attitudes in the passages. On the chalkboard make two columns where students can take turns recording the contrasting attitudes they see reflected in the verses. (Example: trust/worry, contentment/greed, asking God/thinking God doesn't care.) Conclude this step by asking, **What did you learn about God? What did you learn about yourself? What did you learn about your communication with God?**

Step 2: Divide class into three groups. Each group may choose one of the following ways to summarize an important idea from *Step 1:* write new lyrics to a familiar tune; write a rap; write a short poem. After students are ready, have each group perform for the rest of the class. Remind them that as they perform, their words can encourage the others in the class to trust God for the things they need.

Step 3: Same as *Step 3* in original Exploration.

CONCLUSION

Choose a Conclusion activity to help students express themselves in prayer to God the provider.

CONCLUSION(3-5 minutes)

Materials needed: Copies for each student of "Make Your Own Request" Student Worksheet, pencils.

Ask your students to complete the "Make Your Own Request" worksheet. Encourage them to work independently and thoughtfully. Close in prayer, thanking God for taking care of His children.

ALTERNATE CONCLUSION(7-10 minutes)

Materials needed: Bibles, paper, pencils.

Distribute Bibles, paper and pencils to each student. Ask them to turn to Matthew 6:9-11 in their Bibles. Then instruct students to write an amplified version of the first half of the Lord's Prayer, personalizing it with their own thoughts. Direct their thinking by providing an example of the first part of the passage:

Dear God, I know you are my Father and you love me. Your heavenly home is a place that is hard for me to even imagine, but you are still here, close to me. The sound of your name is special and very sacred to me. It makes me aware of how great you are.

Emphasize that the students' prayers are to contain their own thoughts, using Jesus' words as just an outline.

Allow volunteers to share what they have written. (Be prepared to share your own in case students are hesitant to share.) Close in prayer, thanking God for His care and asking for the willingness to help care for others.

EXTRA FEATURES

Add one or more of these features to your session to increase friendship and impact:

Worship—see page 6.
Games—see page 49.
Munchies—see page 48.
Crafts—see page 50.

Forgive Us Our Debts

KEY VERSE
And forgive us our debts, as we forgive our debtors. Matthew 6:12 (*KJV*)

BIBLICAL BASIS
Psalm 103:12; Matthew 6:14,15;18:21-35; Ephesians 4:32; Hebrews 8:12

FOCUS OF THE SESSION
Since our heavenly Father has forgiven us, we must also forgive others.

AIMS OF THIS SESSION
During this session each learner will:
- RETELL the story of the unforgiving servant;
- DESCRIBE three steps that will help us forgive others;
- PLAN a way to show forgiveness.

TEACHER'S BIBLE STUDY

God Forgives Us

The most beautiful truth of the Christian faith is that God sent His Son to save us from our sins. His love is unconditional, but His forgiveness is not.

To be forgiven for the first time and become Christians we must recognize that sin separates us from God who is holy. On our own, we cannot hope to achieve the righteousness necessary to fellowship with the Creator. In fact the penalty for sin is death—spiritual separation from God (Rom. 6:23). But this penalty was paid by Jesus on the cross. By accepting Jesus' sacrifice and turning from sinfulness we can be reconciled with God (Rom. 3:22-24).

Once in the family of God, fellowship with Him is possible, and His love is enjoyed for eternity. However, there still remains a continuing need to be forgiven and to learn to forgive others. In today's lesson we will learn about sin and forgiveness.

Different Kinds of Sin

In the New Testament there are five different words for sin. The first one means to miss the mark. It is the sin of failing to be what we might have been or would have been. It is a picture of an archer at target practice who cannot, no matter how carefully he takes aim, hit the bull's eye. In fact, he cannot even hit the target. *For all have sinned and fall short of the glory of God* (Rom. 3:23). No matter how good a person may be, the fact remains—everyone is a sinner.

The second word for sin means stepping across a line which is drawn between right and wrong. If we remain on one side of the line we offend no one. When we cross over the line we get in trouble. But it is human nature to step across that line—to touch the wall with the "wet paint" sign just to see if the paint is really wet. So often we find ourselves with paint on our fingers.

"Slipping across" is another meaning for sin in the New Testament. It is not the deliberate act of "stepping across" but more like hitting an icy spot on the road. It can be avoided if we are always on guard but so often we are swept away by an impulse or some passion. Even the most cautious can lose his or her self-control and slip into sin.

A fourth word for sin means lawlessness. This is the act of knowing the law and yet breaking the law. It starts as one of the most familiar of all human traits—to do what we like. It leads to defying the law.

The last word for sin is the one used in the Lord's Prayer. It is the word for debt, meaning the failure to pay what is due when it is due. Not one of us has completely given to God and to others what is due them. "Debt" here is not limited to a monetary or material meaning. It can refer to attitudes such as appreciation, kindness, caring, serving, etc. Such human perfection does not exist and is the source of separation from the Father and the people in our lives.

Forgive Us Our Debts

If we follow Jesus' example and pray as He taught us, we find ourselves in God's presence, worshiping His name and wanting to be in His will. As our minds are focused on Him and His glory we are drawn to be a part of His kingdom. With this framework for prayer we become aware of our complete dependence upon Him and it is only natural that we cry out to be forgiven of our debts.

There is nothing we can do to pay back what we owe. There is no reason to try, because Jesus, through His death and resurrection, has made the payment in full already. He came to give His life as a ransom for many. Forgiveness is never earned. It is sought humbly so that a broken relation with God can be restored.

As We Forgive Our Debtors

It is much easier to ask for forgiveness from God than to be the one who does the forgiving. But "forgiving" and "forgiven" are an inseparable pair. Jesus makes it very clear that our desire to be forgiven starts with the willingness to forgive others (see Matt. 6:14,15).

We are commanded in Ephesians 4:32 to *Be kind and compassionate to one another, forgiving each other, just as in Christ God forgave you.* Jesus gave us the supreme example when He prayed from the cross that His executioners be forgiven. Since so great a price was paid for our liberation by Jesus' sacrifice, it is only fitting that we should willingly liberate others by offering our forgiveness.

We are forgiven by grace, not by earning it. But it is not until we forgive others that we experience the true blessing of God's forgiveness. We must make things right with people we can see before we can fully make things right with God, whom we cannot see.

The Unmerciful Servant

Frequently Jesus returned in His teaching to the subject of forgiveness (Matt. 6:14,15; 9:6; Mark 11:25; Luke 6:37; 17:3). When Peter asked Jesus how many times he should forgive someone (Matt. 18:21), Jesus told a vivid parable. His story of the unmerciful servant (Matt. 18:21-35) clearly teaches that an unforgiving person has no hope of forgiveness for him or herself.

The story Jesus told is about a king who, in trying to settle his accounts with his servants, found one of them with a several million dollar debt which he was making little or no effort to repay. The king decided to sell the servant, his family and all his possessions to repay the debt.

The servant begged for more time to pay back what he owed but instead, the merciful king had compassion on the servant and forgave him of the debt.

A short time later the servant who had been forgiven ran across a fellow slave who owed him just a few dollars. Instead of following his master's example by forgiving the debt, this unmerciful man had his fellow servant thrown into jail until he paid back every last cent. When the other servants heard what happened they became outraged and told the king. The king scolded his servant severely and sent him to prison until he could pay off his debt.

Jesus ended the parable with a stern warning—*This is how my heavenly Father will treat each of you unless you forgive your brother from your heart* (Matt. 18:35).

It is quite clear that our heavenly Father is very serious about forgiveness. He made the ultimate sacrifice to forgive the debt we owe, which is far too great for us to pay ourselves. On the cross, Christ paid the bill for our misuse of all God entrusted to us. He paid for the damage done by our self-will and stubborn pride, our greed and evil thoughts. He cancelled the debt we owe. Even the ridiculously-contrasting sums of money owed in the Lord's parable are only a shadow of God's unlimited mercy.

Learning to Forgive

What shall we do? How shall we learn to forgive so that we can experience forgiveness by God? Forgiveness is not an act isolated in time, but a continuing process that daily shapes the way we interact with others. Here are three guidelines to aid a Christian in forgiving another person.

First, we need to commit ouselves to actively forgive the one who wronged us. This must be a conscious, deliberate act of the will. Unless we make the decision to forgive, grievances can pile up. Each of us has sinned against others and been blessed—at times—by the forgiveness of others. As believers, we have been forgiven of our sins through Christ and are, thus, freed to forgive others.

Second, we need to put the offensive act behind us and leave it there. Rather than remembering another's wrongdoing with malice or bitterness, we need to try to put ourselves in the other's shoes, to try to understand why the other acted as he or she did. After all, God has done much more than this for us. *As far as the east is from the west, so far has He removed our transgressions from us* (Ps. 103:12).

Third, we must put the offending person in front of us—by praying for the person and committing him or her to God's care. The love Jesus taught about seeks the highest good for others. It does not take into account what others have done or how they have treated us.

God wants to nurture us and mold us into His likeness. Only through the power of Christ are we enabled to love as we ought to love. Help your students understand that by learning to forgive as God forgives, we learn to love as He would have us love.

Notes

APPROACH

Choose one Approach to help students think about the value of forgiveness.

APPROACH(3-5 minutes)

Materials Needed: A copy for each student of the "Prayer Blocker" Student Worksheet, pencils.

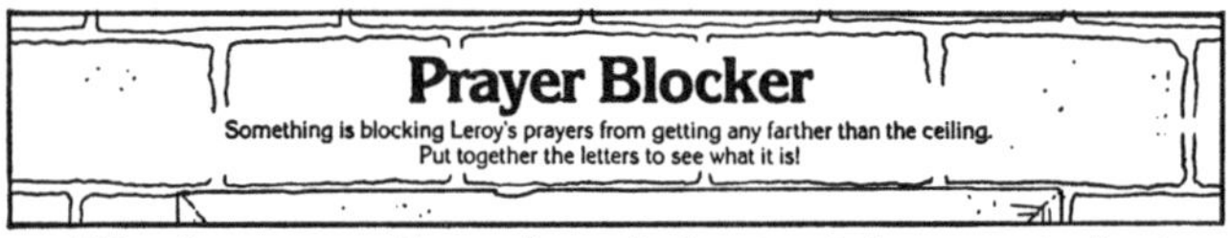

Distribute pencils and worksheets. Ask your students to work individually to figure out the scrambled word puzzle on their "Prayer Blocker" worksheets. (Note: The answer is "not forgiving others.")

Move to the Exploration by saying something like this: **The Bible says,** *If I had cherished sin in my heart, the Lord would not have listened"* (Ps. 66:18). It is wrong to have an unforgiving spirit. As the cartoon on your worksheet shows, an unforgiving spirit can hinder your relationship with God. Let's take a closer look at this subject.

ALTERNATE APPROACH(5-7 minutes)

Materials needed: Copy for each student of the "Hoarder of Hurts" Student Worksheet.

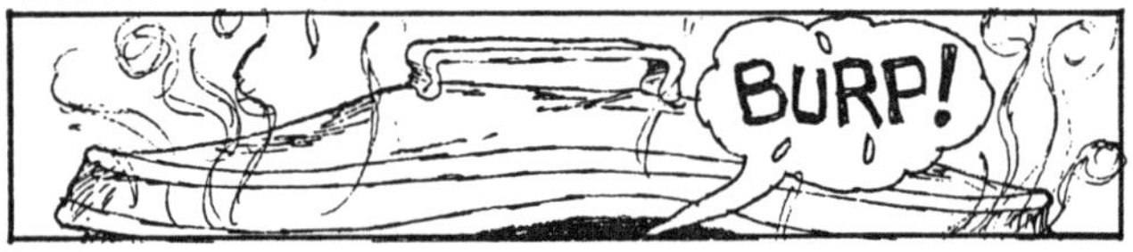

Ask your students to read the "Hoarder of Hurts" poem on their worksheets. After a minute or so, ask your students questions such as: **What do you think this limerick is talking about? What kind of person is the Hoarder of Hurts? What danger is there in being this kind of person?**

Move to the Exploration by saying something like this: **The Hoarder of Hurts is just a silly way of introducing you to a very serious and difficult subject—forgiving other people. Let's take a look at what God has to say about this important subject.**

EXPLORATION

Choose an Exploration to help your students understand that because God forgives us, we should also forgive others.

EXPLORATION(55-60 minutes)

Materials needed: Bibles, dictionary, paper, pencils, butcher or shelf paper, felt pens, newsprint, chalkboard and chalk.

Step 1: Distribute Bibles. Have students read Matthew 6:12 aloud. Then ask a volunteer to look up the definitions of "forgive" in the dictionary and read them to the class. Have another volunteer write the definitions on the chalkboard. Ask, **What do you think Jesus meant when He said, *Forgive us our debts, as we forgive our debtors?*** Have another volunteer look up the definitions of "debt" and "debtors."

Step 2: Divide your class into groups of three or four students. Select from the ideas below one activity for all groups to do or assign a different activity to each group. Make sure to give students a specific time limit in which to work (20-30 minutes) and the proper materials and workspace in which to get the job done.

Group 1: Read Matthew 18:21-35 and draw a mural of the events contained in this passage.

Group 2: Read Matthew 18:21-35 and create a short drama, pantomime or skit that shows what took place in this passage.

Group 3: Read Matthew 18:21-35 and create an 8-12 panel cartoon strip for the *Jerusalem Times* Sabbath Edition that would re-tell this story.

Group 4: Read Matthew 18:21-35 and write what might have been the royal court record of the king in this parable.

Ask students to present their work and explain what their projects communicate about forgiveness. Post students' work around the room.

Step 3: Ask your entire group these questions: **Who did the king symbolize in the parable? The servant? Why do you think the servant ordered his debtor to pay up? In what way are you like the unforgiving servant? What does this story teach you about God? What is the debt we owe to God? How did God forgive us of our debt? What must we do to have that forgiveness? What does this parable teach us to do once we have been forgiven by God? Based on the Lord's Prayer and this story, how important is it that we forgive others? Why?**

Move to the Conclusion by saying something like this: **We have seen how God has forgiven us and that we ought to forgive others. But the hard work comes in when we have to get down to the business of actually forgiving. Let's take a minute and consider if there is anyone that you need to straighten things out with this week.**

ALTERNATE EXPLORATION(55-60 minutes)

Materials needed: Tape recorder(s), blank cassette tape(s), Bibles, copy for each student of the "Forgive-O-Meter" Student Worksheet, pencils, paper.

Step 1: Lead a short discussion concerning those things for which we often need forgiveness. Distribute worksheets. Working in pairs, have students come to a consensus about the things that would be hardest to forgive, then record them on the "Forgive-O-Meter" chart. Ask each pair to share their conclusions with the group.

Step 2: Divide your class into groups of three or four and distribute Bibles, pencils, paper, a tape recorder and tape to each group. Read Matthew 6:12 aloud, then ask a good reader to read aloud Matthew 18:21-35. Instruct each group to recreate the parable as a radio drama. Encourage students to write a script for the drama and to practice before they record. (You may wish to provide a variety of noisemakers for sound effects.)

Allow each group to go into a separate room to plan and record their drama. Then bring students back together and play back the results to the whole group.

Step 3: Same as *Step 3* in original Exploration.

Move to the Conclusion by saying something like this: **We have seen that God freely forgives us, and we should therefore be willing to forgive others. When we have an attitude of forgiveness, we get along better with others and we can pray with a clear conscience. Let's spend a moment thinking about who we might need to forgive this week.**

CONCLUSION

CONCLUSION(5-7 minutes)

Choose a Conclusion activity to help students identify situations when they need to show forgiveness.

Materials needed: Paper, pencils, chalk, chalkboard.

Letter the word "FORGIVE" on the chalkboard and say: **We have learned that when someone hurts us God wants us to forgive him or her, but have you ever tried to forgive someone? It can be a hard thing to do! Let's talk about three steps that will help you forgive others.**

Pass out paper and pencils. As you lead your students through the three steps involved in forgiveness, draw this sketch on chalkboard or poster paper.

Direct the students to copy the sketch on their papers as you are drawing it. As you draw the stick figure say, **Each of us has had a situation in our lives in which someone has wronged us. If we want to obey God and forgive that person we must first make the decision to forgive.** As you write DECIDE say, **First, we must decide that we are going to forgive the person who wronged us. If we never decide to forgive, we won't forgive.** As you write ACT say, **After deciding to forgive we need to put the act behind us. That means we no longer dwell on the act of wrongdoing or the hurt it caused us. The Bible says, *As far as the east is from the west, so far has he removed our transgressions from us*** (Ps. 103:12). **We follow God's example as we put the act behind us.** As you write PERSON say, **Third, we put the person who hurt us in front of us. Sometimes when we are hurt, our first reaction is often to have nothing to do with that person anymore. But when we forgive it is important not to shut out a person. Instead we can put the person in front of us by praying for and showing love to him or her. Again, we are following Christ's example who loves and forgives us even when we don't deserve it.**

Have students turn over their papers and write down a recent situation in which someone hurt them. Lead the students in a prayer by saying something like, **Imagine the situation in which you were hurt by another. Are you willing to decide to forgive? If so, silently tell God now. Now imagine that you are putting the wrongdoing and hurt behind you, choosing not to dwell on it. Now imagine that you are putting that person in front of you. Silently pray for that person now.**

ALTERNATE CONCLUSION(7-10 minutes)

Materials needed: Paper, pencils, fine-tip felt pens.

To begin, you may want to explain the three steps that help us forgive (see original Conclusion).

Distribute paper, pencils and felt pens. Have students fold paper so it is divided into fourths, then number each square. Ask each student to create a cartoon depicting his or her own personal forgiveness story. It should include a plan for forgiving a specific person. Each student should draw pictures of: Square 1—a time he or she sinned and needed forgiveness; Square 2—God forgiving him or her; Square 3—a specific situation when someone did wrong to him or her; Square 4—a way he or she plans to show forgiveness to that person.

When students' drawings are completed, have volunteers explain one or more of their cartoons to the class. Close in prayer, allowing students to pray for God's help in forgiving others.

EXTRA FEATURES

Add one or more of these features to your session to increase friendship and impact:

Worship—see page 6.
Games—see page 49.
Munchies—see page 48.
Crafts—see page 50.

Lead Us Not into Temptation

KEY VERSE

And lead us not into temptation, but deliver us from evil. For thine is the kingdom, and the power, and the glory, forever. Amen. Matthew 6:13 (*KJV*)

BIBLICAL BASIS

Psalm 119:11; Proverbs 1:10; Matthew 4:1-11;26:41; 1 Corinthians 10:13; Philippians 4:13

FOCUS OF THE SESSION

God can protect us from Satan's temptations as we live in obedience to His word.

AIMS OF THIS SESSION

During this session each learner will:

- NAME ways students his or her age are tempted;
- LIST what a Christian can do to fortify against temptation;
- IDENTIFY vulnerable areas in his or her own life.

TEACHER'S BIBLE STUDY

Tested and Tried

In the final petition of the Lord's Prayer it appears that Jesus is suggesting God will tempt us unless we ask Him not to. However, we can look at other places in the Scriptures to see that God does not tempt anyone (Jas. 1:13) and that we can count it as joy to go through trials such as temptation (Jas. 1:2). What then is Jesus saying?

This petition, "And lead us not into temptation, but deliver us from evil," is actually two different ways of saying the same thing. For Christians, our focus should not be on the temptations brought to us by Satan, the evil one, but on God's ability to deliver us from the traps Satan sets.

The word temptation can best be expressed as a trial or test that refines and strengthens. When we are tested, it is for the purpose of being delivered, and becoming stronger people because of the test. God does not forsake His children in the midst of their trials but provides a way of escape (1 Cor. 10:13).

If we have sincerely prayed for forgiveness, then our longings should reflect a desire not to sin again—to be "delivered." It is important for your students to know that even though they will continue at times to struggle in their obedience to God, they should never accept failure as final or as a surrender to sin.

Your students are familiar with being tempted. Although they may be old enough to know what "gets them," they are not experienced enough to know HOW they are tempted or how to stand fast against the assaults of temptations. This lesson will give them the opportunity to see that we were made by God for victory, not for defeat. The Bible says that God *is able to keep you from falling and to present you before his glorious presence without fault and with great joy* (Jude 24). It is Satan's lie that says we are just human and have to be defeated by sin.

Practically everything we have or will encounter can become a source of temptation for us. What makes it so difficult for young people is that most temptations are very visible and accessible and are made to appear so enticing by the media and by peers. Because of their vulnerability and lack of experience in knowing how to stand firm, your students need to be shown where temptation will usually come from and they definitely need to learn defenses against it.

The Attack of Temptation

There is no better illustration of resisting temptation than that of Jesus in the wilderness (Matt. 4:1-11). We are told that He was led by the Spirit into the wilderness for the purpose of being tempted by Satan.

We read that Jesus was first confronted where He was most vulnerable. After fasting for 40 days, Jesus must have been close to starvation. At this point Satan suggested to Jesus that He could turn the stones into bread to meet His physical need. What we see here is that physical needs are a primary source of temptation.

Each person has his or her own weaknesses and these are the points at which temptation strikes. While it may seem that the attack of physical temptation is impossible to resist, you can comfort your students with the knowledge that Jesus suffered in His temptations and He is able to help those who are being tempted (Heb. 2:18).

After failing in his first attempt, Satan tempted Jesus a second time by trying to persuade Him to prove Himself in front of other people. He asserted that if Jesus were the Son of God, He could jump off the Temple and not be hurt because the angels would take care of Him.

Many kids feel constant pressure to measure up to their friends' expectations. They would rather make the kind of leap Jesus refused than to risk being rejected by their peers. Augustine said that he made himself worse than he was so that he would not be looked down upon. Strange as it seems, your students may also go to that extreme to be accepted.

Satan's final temptation was his offer to Jesus of everything He came to earth for in the first place. Satan told Jesus the glory and power could be His now, without the physical pain of the cross. He wanted Jesus to compromise by using a different means to the end God had planned for Him. He took Jesus to a high mountain and showed Him all the kingdoms of the world and said they would be His if Jesus worshiped him.

A major source of temptation for your students is the enticement of the world and its promise of glory that distracts them and pulls them away from God. The world tempts us with the invitation to be powerful, to put ourselves at the center and worship anything that makes us strong.

In each recorded instance of specific temptation, Jesus combated Satan with the Word of God. We can follow His example. The Bible teaches that we are to hide the Word in our heart so that we won't sin against God (Ps. 119:11).

Deliver Us from Evil

In John 17:15 Jesus prayed that His disciples not be taken out of the world but that God protect them from the evil one. We can rest in the knowledge that Jesus will intercede for us and protect us from the enemy. But God also expects us to ask Him to keep us safe from the enemy's hand. By praying, "but deliver us from evil," we are emphasizing our need for God's help to be kept free of sin.

The evil spoken of here is not an impersonal wickedness out there somewhere. Rather, it is the evil one. Satan is the personal power of evil and it is his aim to separate us from God and thwart every effort we make to live a holy and acceptable life.

To pray for deliverance does not mean we will be exempt from testing. It does not imply escape, but victory. We are asking for a hedge around us so that we can be protected from naked exposure to Satan's attacks.

Resisting Temptation

There are some specific steps your students can take that will help them resist temptation. One of the greatest defenses is simply to determine to be good. This will require a measure of self-respect and courage, both of which result from your students realizing that they are children of God—they have been adopted by Him.

A child of God also finds it easier to resist temptation by remembering people he or she loves and focusing on not causing them pain.

An active, consistent prayer life also serves to strengthen your students' ability to resist temptation. Jesus said in the garden to *watch and pray so that you will not fall into temptation* (Matt. 26:41).

Your students' prayer time should take on some specific disciplines: encourage them to pray daily, to acknowledge God as their Father, and to approach Him as a Holy God. They should also confess wrongdoings and ask forgiveness, and they should ask for strength to meet temptation. They can learn to be steadfast in the One who is stronger than they are and thereby win the victory (1 John 4:4;5:3-5).

Your students will find a strong defense against temptation if they will remember the presence of Jesus Christ in their lives. Jesus promised to be with us always (Matt. 28:20). Teach your class to live as though Jesus is their invited guest at every activity. A basic truth of the Christian faith is that He is beside us always.

The Bible serves as our most powerful defense in the fight against evil and the evil one. The most important habit that any of your students can develop is to spend time reading and memorizing the Word of God every day. God has given us His Word so that we can learn about Him, know about His plan of salvation through the death of His Son, and learn about ourselves and our need for Him. It is by reading the Bible and applying what they read, that your students will gain strength to face temptation. We are told by the psalmist that the way a young person can keep pure is *by living according to your word. I seek you with all my heart; do not let me stray from your commands. I have hidden your word in my heart that I might not sin against you* (Ps. 119:9-11).

The Lord wants to answer this prayer by transforming us into the image of His dear Son. We gradually become more recognizable as members of His family into which He has adopted us. Therefore to Him only belongs the power and the glory forever.

Notes

APPROACH

Choose an Approach to direct students' thinking toward areas of temptation in their lives.

APPROACH(5-7 minutes)

Materials needed: Cardboard shoe box with lid, index cards, felt pens, scissors.

Preparation: Make a slit in the lid of the cardboard box. Place cards and felt pens on a table.

As students arrive for class instruct them to write on an index card some ways kids their age are tempted. They do not have to sign their names. Have students insert their cards into the shoe box. Read several of the cards aloud to the class.

Make transition to next part of lesson by saying something like this: **Even though many of us are Christians and know the difference between right and wrong, we are often tempted to do wrong. Today we will be looking at the ways God can help us *not* give in to temptation but live in obedience to Him.**

ALTERNATE APPROACH(5-7 minutes)

Materials needed: Felt pens, large sheets of paper, index cards, pencils.

Preparation: Write each "temptation phrase" listed below on a sheet of paper—one phrase on each sheet of paper, scrambling the letters in each word (see sketch). The "temptation phrases" are: tell a dirty joke, laugh at someone, gossip about someone, cheat on a test, steal money, kick the dog, lie to parents, yell at sister, look at dirty magazines, copy friend's homework, try drugs, eat chocolate, vegetate in front of the TV.

Post phrases on the walls around the room. Give each student an index card and a pencil. When a signal is given, students race to see who can unscramble the phrases first. Explain that each phrase is something that they may have been tempted to do. When five minutes are up, students must stop working. Review students' answers.

Make transition to next part of lesson by saying: **All people are tempted to sin, even grown-ups like me.** (Give a specific example from your own life to help your students feel open about sharing.) **How many of you were tempted to sin in at least one of these ways this week? The good news is that in the Bible God provides guidelines that will help us obey Him more and give in to temptation less. That's what we're going to talk about today.**

EXPLORATION

Choose one of the Explorations to help students discover what Christians can do to fortify against temptations.

EXPLORATION(50-60 minutes)

Materials needed: Bibles, pencils, index cards, tape, copies of the "What's the Diff?" Student Worksheet, scissors, a game marker for each student; for every group of four students—"Sticky Situations Game" Student Worksheets and a number cube.

Preparation: Cut apart the game cards for each "Sticky Situation Game." Tape together the two sheets of each "Sticky Situation Game."

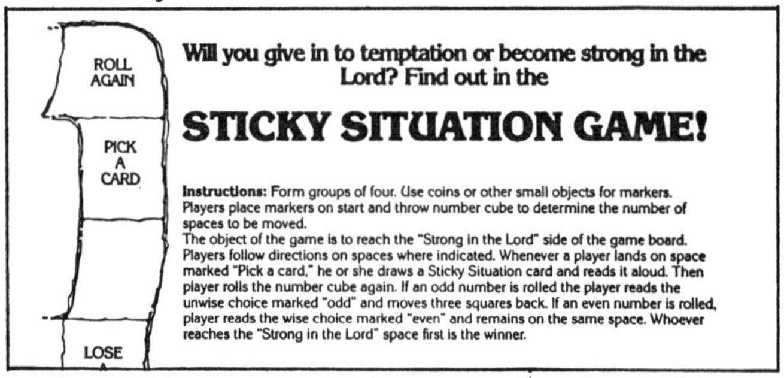

Will you give in to temptation or become strong in the Lord? Find out in the

STICKY SITUATION GAME!

Instructions: Form groups of four. Use coins or other small objects for markers. Players place markers on start and throw number cube to determine the number of spaces to be moved.
The object of the game is to reach the "Strong in the Lord" side of the game board. Players follow directions on spaces where indicated. Whenever a player lands on space marked "Pick a card," he or she draws a Sticky Situation card and reads it aloud. Then player rolls the number cube again. If an odd number is rolled the player reads the unwise choice marked "odd" and moves three squares back. If an even number is rolled, player reads the wise choice marked "even" and remains on the same space. Whoever reaches the "Strong in the Lord" space first is the winner.

Step 1: Divide the class into pairs. Distribute Bibles, pencils and index cards to each pair. Ask them to look up Matthew 6:13 and write the verse on the index card using more contemporary language. Tell them to communicate the meaning of the verse without using any of the key words (nouns, verbs) that are found in their Bibles. Encourage each pair to share their version of the verse with the class.

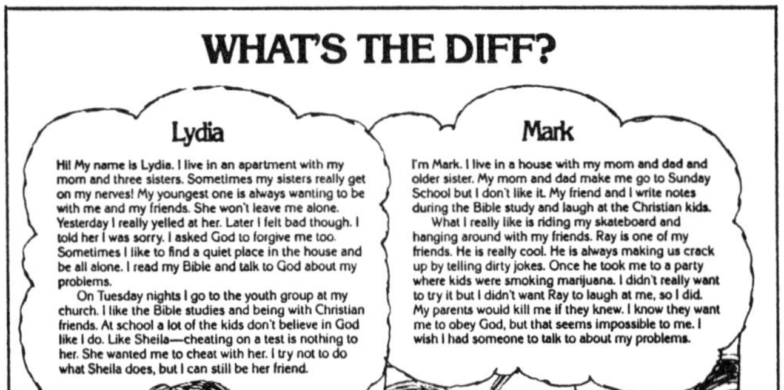

WHAT'S THE DIFF?

Lydia

Hi! My name is Lydia. I live in an apartment with my mom and three sisters. Sometimes my sisters really get on my nerves! My youngest one is always wanting to be with me and my friends. She won't leave me alone. Yesterday I really yelled at her. Later I felt bad though. I told her I was sorry. I asked God to forgive me too. Sometimes I like to find a quiet place in the house and be all alone. I read my Bible and talk to God about my problems.

On Tuesday nights I go to the youth group at my church. I like the Bible studies and being with Christian friends. At school a lot of the kids don't believe in God like I do. Like Sheila—cheating on a test is nothing to her. She wanted me to cheat with her. I try not to do what Sheila does, but I can still be her friend.

Mark

I'm Mark. I live in a house with my mom and dad and older sister. My mom and dad make me go to Sunday School but I don't like it. My friend and I write notes during the Bible study and laugh at the Christian kids.

What I really like is riding my skateboard and hanging around with my friends. Ray is one of my friends. He is really cool. He is always making us crack up by telling dirty jokes. Once he took me to a party where kids were smoking marijuana. I didn't really want to try it but I didn't want Ray to laugh at me, so I did. My parents would kill me if they knew. I know they want me to obey God, but that seems impossible to me. I wish I had someone to talk to about my problems.

Step 2: Distribute "What's the Diff?" Student Worksheets. Ask for two volunteers to each read aloud one of the stories. Say, **Both Lydia and Mark faced temptations in their lives. Why do you think Mark**

gave into temptation more often than Lydia did? God has given us guidelines in His word to help us withstand temptations. Read aloud each verse on the worksheet and have students write down how Lydia followed the guideline of each verse and how Mark did not.

Step 3: Have students form groups of four. Give each group a "Sticky Situations Game" worksheet, a set of game cards, a number cube and markers. Players take turns rolling number cube and moving markers. Any player who lands on a "Pick a Card" space draws a card and reads it aloud. Player then rolls number cube again. If an odd number is rolled, player reads appropriate answer on card and moves back three squares. If an even number is rolled the player reads appropriate answer on card and remains on the same space. Student who reaches the "Strong in the Lord" space first is the winner.

Step 4: After game has been played, call on several volunteers to comment on tempting situations they have faced. Lead the group in suggesting practical ways to avoid and overcome temptation. Share ideas from the Teacher's Bible Study.

ALTERNATE EXPLORATION(50-60 minutes)

Materials needed: Bibles, paper, pencils, index cards, magazine picture of Junior High-aged girl.

Preparation: Letter the words to the Lord's Prayer (Matt. 6:9-13) on index cards—two or three words on each card. Make a complete set of cards for every three or four students.

Step 1: Divide class into groups of three or four. Give each group a set of index cards on which the words to the Lord's Prayer have been written. Instruct students to mix up the cards. When a signal is given, the groups race to see who can put the passage in order first.

Step 2: Letter the words to the following verses on the chalkboard or overhead transparency: Psalm 119:9,10; Proverbs 1:10; 1 John 1:9; Philippians 4:13; 1 Thessalonians 5:17. Assign a verse to each group of four students by whispering the reference to them. Instruct each group to read their verse and create a modern-day skit showing ways that obeying that verse would help them resist temptation. Allow each group to present their skit to the class. After each skit ask, **Which verse did this skit illustrate? How did following the verse's advice help the person obey God rather than give in to temptation?**

Step 3: Hold up the magazine picture and say, **This is Worried Wilma. Wilma is worried because she can't seem to stop sinning and she doesn't know what to do. She would like to stop sinning but she feels like it is hopeless.** Distribute Bibles. Instruct students to look up and read 1 Corinthians 10:13. Lead class in a discussion of the truth taught in that verse and in Matthew 6:13. Direct students to identify ideas that might help Wilma avoid temptation. Share ideas from Teacher's Bible Study.

CONCLUSION

Choose a Conclusion activity to help students identify vulnerable areas in their lives.

CONCLUSION(7-10 minutes)

Materials needed: Paper, pencils, envelopes, postage stamps.

Distribute paper, envelopes, stamps and pencils. Say, **Each of us wants to obey God and stay close to Him. Without that desire we cannot learn how to resist temptations. The next step in resisting temptation is recognizing when we are usually tempted to sin. The third step is having a plan of what to do when faced with the situation. Imagine you are your own best friend. Your friend has been watching your life and has noticed when you usually are tempted to do wrong. He or she is going to write you a letter now and give you some advice on how you might avoid that temptation in the future.** Have students write letters, then address and stamp them. Collect the letters and mail them sometime during the next week to remind the students how they can resist temptation.

Close in prayer. Allow students to pray for God's help in resisting temptation.

ALTERNATE CONCLUSION(5-7 minutes)

Materials needed: Copies of the "Tangled Up?" Student Worksheet, pencils.

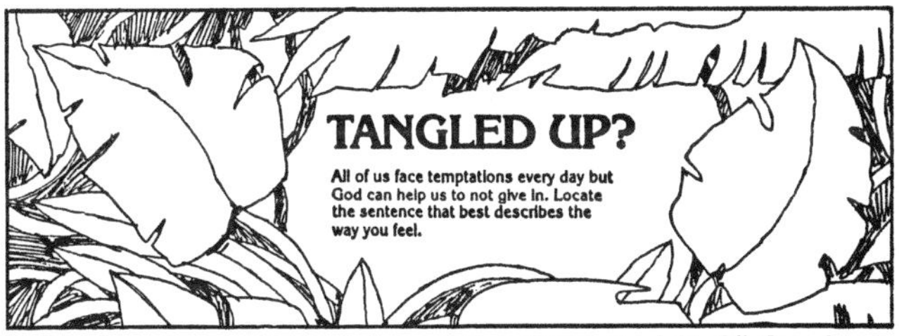

Ask your students to read the "Tangled Up?" Student Worksheet and prayerfully think about their own attitudes. Encourage them to be honest as they find the sentence that best describes the way they feel.

Close in prayer. Give an opportunity for any kids who are caught in a particularly tough situation to stick around and talk.

EXTRA FEATURES

Add one or more of these features to your session to increase friendship and impact:

Worship—see page 6.
Games—see page 49.
Munchies—see page 48.
Crafts—see page 50.

Knowing God

KEY VERSE

I am the good shepherd; I know my sheep and my sheep know me. John 10:14

BIBLICAL BASIS

Psalm 19:8; 25:4; 34:8; 116:1,2; 119:15,16,28,130; 120:1; 145:18; John 10:14; Ephesians 6:18; Philippians 4:6; 2 Timothy 3:16,17

FOCUS OF THE SESSION

It is not enough to know about God; He wants us to have a personal relationship with Him.

AIMS OF THIS SESSION

During this session each learner will:

- CONTRAST knowing about God and having a personal relationship with Him;
- EXAMINE ways we develop a relationship with God through Bible study and prayer;
- SPEND time with God in Bible study and prayer.

TEACHER'S BIBLE STUDY

Knowing vs. Knowing

Many people treat God like a celebrity. They agree that He's important. They know some things about Him. They may even enjoy reading or hearing about Him. They are impressed by someone who has been close to Him. They even enjoy thinking about Him from time to time. But they have no realistic expectation of ever getting to know Him personally. He is far removed from their daily living, like someone on the cover of *People.*

Settling for mere surface knowledge about God seems rather empty when compared with all the rich possibilities of becoming intimately acquainted with Him. Imagine a hungry person gazing at a table filled with delicious food. The person's eyes take in the color and tempting appearance of each morsel. The person's nose is aware of the aroma wafting from the table. Whatever enjoyment these senses bring is nothing compared to actually tasting the food. Unfortunately, many people settle for gathering information about God or observing evidence of God, but never respond to the psalmist's invitation to *taste and see that the Lord is good* (Ps. 34:8).

Many young people attend church regularly, hearing and seeing many things about God without ever entering into a personal relationship with Him. Some may have participated in every session of this course, gaining information about God's attributes, even believing all the truths that have been shared, without ever taking a step to draw closer to Him. They are part of the group, but they miss out on the deep reality of God's presence in their lives.

It is not enough merely to be concerned about those who settle for less than God's best. We must also recognize that Scripture views such a condition as one of great danger. Paul wrote a vivid warning to Timothy about those *having a form of godliness but denying its power* (2 Tim. 3:5).

The person who goes through religious motions without the inner reality is grouped by Paul with a collection of unsavory character traits: *lovers of themselves, lovers of money, boastful, proud, abusive, disobedient to their parents, ungrateful, unholy, without love, unforgiving, slanderous, without self-control, brutal, not lovers of the good, treacherous, rash, conceited, lovers of pleasure rather than lovers of God* (2 Tim. 3:2-4). There is something deadly about settling for the outer trappings of faith.

Your students need to know that the knowledge they have about God is of no value—and may even be harmful—if they do not act on the knowledge and begin getting to know God in a personal way.

It's a Relationship

You may have some students in your group who have taken initial steps toward God, but do not feel that they are making much progress in getting to know Him better. They have accepted Christ as Savior, but have not yet discovered a daily sense of Him as Friend. Think about someone with whom you have a close relationship. How did you develop that kind of relationship? No doubt you have spent many hours together. You have observed one another in many different circumstances. You have shared experiences of joy and of pain. You've had fun times and serious times. You've spent time talking and listening. Each of you has given and received. In the Bible we discover that God desires this kind of intimate relationship with His people. He wants to communicate with us and He wants us to communicate with Him. God wants to give to us and wants us to respond by giving back to Him. This session is designed to encourage your students to develop an ongoing personal relationship with God, beginning with the basics of Bible study and prayer.

God Reaches Out to Us

Psalm 119:130 says, *The entrance of your words gives light; it gives understanding to the simple.* Through His Word, God is communicating with us. As we listen and meditate on it, we receive light and understanding. Through the Scriptures, God teaches, rebukes, corrects and trains us (2 Tim. 3:16,17). Through His Word we receive strength in weariness and sorrow (Ps. 119:28). We receive joy (Ps. 19:8). God reaches out to us through His Word. We reach out to Him by reading it, seeking to understand it and applying it to our lives. Psalm 119:15,16 tells what our response to God's Word should be: *I meditate on your precepts and consider your ways. I delight in your decrees; I will not neglect your word.* Bible study is an essential element in developing a close relationship with God.

We Reach Out to God

Another beautiful way God has provided for us to interact with Him is prayer. Psalm 116:1,2 says, *I love the Lord, for he heard my voice; he heard my cry for mercy. Because he turned his ear to me, I will call on him as long as I live.* We talk to God and He listens. He not only listens but responds to our requests. Psalm 120:1 says, *I call on the Lord in my distress, and he answers me.*

Ephesians 6:18 instructs us to pray all kinds of prayers and Philippians 4:6 tells us to pray about everything. In other words, God wants us to communicate with Him about all aspects of our lives. Not only can we tell Him our needs and troubles, but we may seek Him and gain an understanding of His ways. In Psalm 25:4 David prayed, *Show me your ways, O Lord, teach me your paths.*

After spending time talking with friends and listening to them, we feel closer to them. In the same way, God promises to be near to us when we seek Him in prayer. *The Lord is near to all who call on him* (Ps. 145:18).

We're Not Alone

It is important to remember that we are not alone in seeking to build a relationship with God. God has designed the body of Christ so that each member contributes to the growth of the others. For younger Christians it is especially important to be in contact with mature believers who can teach and model the Christian life. Ephesians 4:11-13 says, *It was he who gave some to be apostles, some to be prophets, some to be evangelists, and some to be pastors and teachers, to prepare God's people for works of service, so that the body of Christ may be built up until we all reach unity in the faith and in the knowledge of the son of God and become mature, attaining to the whole measure of the fullness of Christ.*

As you encourage your students to build their own personal relationships with God, remind them that at the same time they need to build relationships with other believers. They will not only find encouragement, but protection from heading the wrong direction in their walk with the Lord.

Hebrews 10:25 says, *Let us not give up meeting together, as some are in the habit of doing, but let us encourage one another—and all the more as you see the Day approaching.* This session provides the opportunity for you to teach and encourage your students by sharing personally from your own life. There are also opportunities for your students to encourage each other as together they strive toward the goal of growing closer to Christ.

Notes

APPROACH

Select an Approach to help students become aware of the difference between knowing about someone and having a relationship with that person.

APPROACH(5-10 minutes)

Materials needed: "Guess My Celebrity" Student Worksheet, pencils.

Distribute copies of the "Guess My Celebrity" worksheet. Have students work individually, writing clues to describe a celebrity. After two or three minutes, call time and invite each student to read the clues he or she wrote. You may want to give a prize to the student who makes the most correct guesses.

If you have more than eight or ten students in your class, divide into groups of five or six. Have students in each group read their clues to each other. Have each group then decide on one set of clues to read to the rest of the class.

Lead into the Exploration by asking, **Do any of you personally know the celebrity you described? What is the difference between knowing *about* someone and knowing him or her personally?** After several students have responded, point out that today's session emphasizes our need to learn to know God, not just know about Him.

ALTERNATE APPROACH(5-7 minutes)

Materials needed: Chalkboard and chalk or overhead projector, blank transparency and transparency pen.

Ask an outgoing, well-liked member of your group to come to the front of the room. Ask the group members to imagine that they were just meeting this person for the first time. **What are some first impressions that could make you think you might like to know this person better?** Expect some smart cracks from the group, but try to build a reasonable list of appealing qualities to write on the chalkboard or overhead.

Next, ask the group to suggest actions they could take to get to know this "new" person better. List these ideas also, even the ones that are off-the-wall. Then thank your "volunteer" for being a good sport.

Lead into the Bible Exploration by pointing out that getting to know God is not all that different from getting to know another person. Ask the group to suggest some of the qualities of God they know. List these attributes in place of those describing your "volunteer." Then explain that this session deals with very practical ways to get to know God better.

EXPLORATION

Choose an Exploration that will help your students discover ways Bible study and prayer strengthen our relationship with God.

EXPLORATION(40-50 minutes)

Materials needed: Paper, pencils, copies for each student of the "Close Encounters With God" Student Worksheet, poster with words of John 10:14 lettered on it, watch with a second hand.

Step 1: Have class form groups of five or six and sit on chairs in circles. Show the poster of John 10:14 and have class read it several times together until the students have it memorized. Then instruct students to practice saying it in their groups in this way: The first person stands, says the first word of the verse and then quickly sits down, the next person in the circle stands and says the second word, etc. After the groups have had time to practice, time each group. You may want to give the quickest group a small prize. Then say, **Tell me what you think the verse means. What is the shepherd confident of? Who do the shepherd and the sheep represent? How do the sheep and the shepherd get to know each other?**

Step 2: Pass out paper and pencils. Ask students to think of a person with whom they have a close relationship. Have them draw a line down the center of the page creating two columns. In the first column have the students list things he or she has done to build a relationship with that person. In the second column list things the other person has done to build the relationship. Allow students to share some of their answers. Say, **Now let's discover some ways that we can build a close relationship with God.**

Step 3: Pass out copies of "Close Encounters with God" Student Worksheet. Ask each student to find a partner. Say, **Each of you has someone you feel close to—whether it is a family member, teacher, or a friend. Did you know God wants to have a close relationship with you, too? He knows you better than anyone else ever could and He wants you to know Him. He wants to communicate with you. He wants you to communicate with Him. Let's study some Bible verses and see how God has planned for this communication to take place.** Have students read each verse and write in the first column ways God communicates with us. In the second column students write the things we do to communicate with God. Allow students to share their answers.

ALTERNATE EXPLORATION (40-50 minutes)

Materials needed: Bibles, poster board, felt pens, paper, chalkboard, chalk, slips of paper lettered with these Scripture references: Psalm 25:4,5; Psalm 119:130; Psalm 120:1; Psalm 145:18; 2 Timothy 3:16; poster board, felt pens, paper.

Step 1: Same as *Step 1* of original Exploration.

Step 2: Have class form small groups. Distribute Bibles and a slip of paper with Scripture references to each group. Have each group read their verse and discuss what the verse teaches about two questions: How does God communicate with us? How do we communicate with God?

Step 3: Still in groups, students choose a way to present to the class what they learned about communicating with God. They can make an illustration, perform a skit, or compose a song or poem. When each group is ready, gather class together and have groups present what they learned. Make two lists on the chalkboard. After each presentation write ways God communicates with us on one list and ways we communicate with God on the other list. Say, **What is the main way God communicates with us?** Allow students to respond. **God speaks to us through His Word. If you feel far away from God, if you feel you don't know Him very well, you can do something about it. You can read His Word and talk to Him about what you read. It's up to you if you want to get closer to God.**

CONCLUSION

Choose a Conclusion that will motivate your students to spend time building their relationship with God.

CONCLUSION (10-15 minutes)

Materials needed: Bibles, copies for each student of the "Together Time Journal" Student Worksheet, staplers, pencils, scissors.

Say, **Now you know that you need to read the Bible and pray in order to build your relationship with God—but you may not know where to start.** At this point, share ways you have grown closer to the Lord through Bible study and prayer.

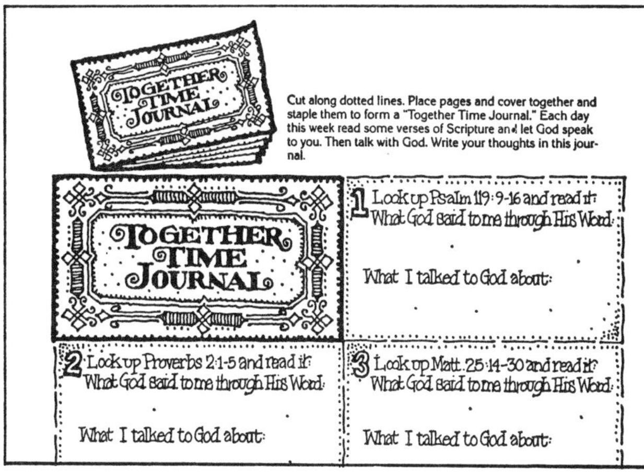

Hand out worksheets, scissors and staplers to students. Have students cut on dotted lines, and staple pages together to form a "Together Time Journal." Say, **Today we have learned that God wants to have a close relationship with us. We can choose to take Him up on that. If we want a close relationship with Him we must spend time each day letting Him speak to us through His Word and speaking to Him through prayer. This journal will help you remember to spend time with God every day this week.** Have students take Bibles and journals and find a place by themselves to spend time with Him right now. Instruct students to read the passage (Ps. 119:9-16) to themselves, think about what they read and then record what God is communicating to them. Next, have students spend time talking to God about the verses and whatever else is on their minds. Instruct the students to write in their journals the things they talked to God about.

ALTERNATE CONCLUSION (10-15 minutes)

Materials needed: Bibles, copy for each student of the "Together Time Journal" Student Worksheet, stapler, pencils, scissors.

Preparation: Assemble one "Together Time Journal" for each student (see instructions in original Conclusion).

Distribute a Bible, pencil and journal to each student. Introduce the journals as in original Conclusion. After students have completed the first page of their journals, have them find partners. Say, **Remember, you are not alone in building a relationship with God. God has made each of us to be a part of the Body of Christ. We are to teach and encourage each other along the way. Take a moment to encourage your partner by sharing what you learned in your "together time" with God.** After partners have had a chance to share, instruct them to exchange phone numbers. During the week partners may want to call each other to see how they're doing on their "together times."

EXTRA FEATURES:

Worship—see page 6.
Games—see page 49.
Munchies—see page 48.
Crafts—see page 50.

The Faithful God

KEY VERSE

God, who has called you into fellowship with his Son Jesus Christ our Lord, is faithful.
1 Corinthians 1:9

BIBLICAL BASIS

Judges 6-7; Psalm 9:10;94:14;121:3,4; Proverbs 2:8;15:29; 1 Corinthians 1:8,9; Philippians 4:19; 1 John 1:9;2:25

FOCUS OF THE SESSION

We can trust God to be faithful in His care for us.

AIMS OF THIS SESSION

During this session each learner will:

- MEMORIZE a passage about God's faithfulness;
- EXAMINE ways God demonstrates His faithfulness;
- THANK God for specific ways He has shown His faithfulness to him or her.

TEACHER'S BIBLE STUDY

God's Faithful Pursuit

The essence of God's faithfulness is that He will not abandon us. This theme runs over and over again through the pages of Scripture. God's faithful and diligent pursuit of our souls has led some writers to call Him the "hound of heaven." He is relentless when it comes to watching after His children. The Bible is replete with accounts of God's loving pursuit of individuals. Let's take a look at two prominent Bible characters who experienced God's persistence.

Consider the prophet Jonah who decided to rebel against the clear will of the Lord. God pursued Jonah all the way to the belly of a fish—and finally Jonah repented. God's faithfulness and Jonah's eventual obedience resulted in one of the biggest revivals in history.

The apostle Paul, who was a firebrand against the gospel was chased down the road to Damascus until the "pharisee of pharisees" gave his heart to the Master. There is no doubt that Paul was singly most responsible for the spread of the gospel and establishment of churches in the first century.

A Caring Shepherd

The parables of Christ also demonstrate the faithful aspect of the Lord. In the parable of the lost sheep Jesus told of a sheep that wandered off and was separated from the safety of the flock. The shepherd cared for each of his sheep, so he left the flock of ninety-nine to go looking for the lost one. The Lord said the shepherd rejoiced when he found the animal and he carried it back to the others. The return of the sheep and the tender care of the shepherd illustrate how God watches out for each of His children (Luke 15:3-7).

Faithfulness can be thought of as continuous attention to someone to ensure the well-being of that individual. God's faithfulness is always demonstrated in the light of His love. He never acts in a manner that does not have our best interests at heart. He will give us what He knows is good for us within the context of eternity. He will give us what we ask for when we are asking for that which is His will.

If you ask a child what he or she would like to eat or drink, you might hear a list consisting of candy, soda, cookies, pastries and other items with little nutritional value. Naturally, a loving parent would not allow a child to eat only this kind of food. Parents give their child what is good for him or her even though the child may not be pleased at the time. If a child requests a dinner of cake, cola and cookies he or she most likely won't get it. If the child asks for an apple for a snack, most of parents would be happy to comply with the request. A parent must do what is best for a child. In the same way, God is faithful to us. He will honor our requests if they are good for us.

The Safety Net

God is the ultimate "safety net." He will protect us from hitting the hard concrete—but sometimes He lets us fall a long way. One who experienced the "long fall" was Job. Job was stripped of all the earthly things that mattered to him and was left with clumsy friends and a nagging wife. Because Job's friends saw a direct connection between a person's actions and the events of life, they tried to identify the sin that brought about Job's great calamity. Job, much to their dismay, insisted that he had been faithful to God and that there were no skeletons hidden in his closet. To proclaim how he trusted the Lord, he declared, *Though He slay me, yet will I hope in him* (Job 13:15).

We are not told what God's full motives were in allowing Job to be put through a living hell. But it is plain to see that Job became a better man because of it. God was faithful to Job even though He allowed catastrophe to hit him. God was faithful to him for Job's ultimate good, even though it was at the expense of all immediate comfort.

It is often because of the experience of heartache and pain that one questions the faithfulness of God. Events can happen that appear void of any good, and immediately God's watchful care is called into question. But God's faithfulness does not mean that bad things will cease happening to us. Rather, we have a Lord who can give us strength to endure and grow through the bad times. *Never will I leave you, never will I forsake you* (Heb. 13:5b).

Mission Impossible

The Bible is full of accounts of individuals who could attest to the faithfulness of God. Often God's faithfulness was shown even when His people lacked faith. One such individual was Gideon. Judges, chapters six and seven, provides an example of the kind of faithfulness that is so typical of God.

Gideon was apprehensive, to say the least, at being called by God, for God's strategy almost seemed to verge on the ridiculous. For Gideon to lead the Israelites in battle against the Midianites appeared to be nothing more than a suicide mission. Time after time God decreased the number of men in Gideon's army to make it perfectly clear that it was God's faithfulness, not Gideon's skill as a general, that would make the difference. God wanted to prove His faithfulness.

One can sympathize with Gideon's early nervousness when he realized that he was heading into battle with a puny number of men and a battle plan that seemed insane. But God did the work for Gideon and so confused the camp of the Midianites that they did all of the fighting—against each other!

God sticks by His children during those times when faith comes hard. *If we are faithless, he will remain faithful, for he cannot disown himself* (2 Tim. 2:13). *For the Lord will not reject his people; he will never forsake his inheritance* (Ps. 94:14).

God stands by His children when times are hard and choices are hard. *He will not let your foot slip—he who watches over you will not slumber; indeed, he who watches over Israel will neither slumber nor sleep* (Ps. 121:3,4).

Trusting His Faithfulness

It probably will not be difficult for the average student in your class to identify with the concept of faithfulness. Many of them have been taken care of all their lives and have been surrounded by those who were faithful to teach and discipline them, love and enjoy them, feed and clothe them. It may not be hard for them to transfer the idea of faithfulness to God because they've had at least one good human model from whom they can transfer the idea. You may even find they so readily accept God's faithfulness that it has no special place in their lives.

The idea of a completely faithful God is important for your students to grasp because there may come a time when they will be let down by human institutions, by friends, by family—even those closest to them. Most of them will at some time experience the feeling of having no one to turn to. But your students will be more prepared to face those times once they have learned of the One who is faithful when all others fail.

God will stick by us and shield us. He will allow to touch us that which will be necessary for our growth and He will catch us when we fall. What then should we do? Trust Him. *Those who know your name will trust in you, for you, Lord, have never forsaken those who seek you* (Ps. 9:10). *Great is your faithfulness* (Lam. 3:23b).

Notes

APPROACH

Choose one Approach to direct students' thinking toward people they can count on to be faithful no matter what.

APPROACH(3-5 minutes)

Say, **Imagine that you are out for a ride on your ten-speed. It is a beautiful day and you are having such a good time that you ride several miles out of town. Suddenly something goes wrong with the gears, leaving the bike inoperable. You are too far from home to walk and your parents are out of town for the day. You have enough money for one phone call in your pocket. When you finally get to a phone, who would you call for assistance and why would you choose that person?**

Ask volunteers to share their answers. Move to the Exploration by saying something like this: **You have given some good reasons why you would choose a particular person to help you when you're in trouble. Each of us would call a person we could count on—someone who wouldn't laugh or leave us stranded. Through our Bible study today we'll see that God is someone we can always trust. We can depend on Him because He is faithful.**

ALTERNATE APPROACH(5-7 minutes)

Ask your students to imagine that they have contracted the disease AIDS through a blood transfusion. Ask them to think of the friends that might still hang out with them if they had this terrible disease.

After taking a moment to think, allow several volunteers to share. Ask, **Why do you think you could count on that person to stick by you?** Move to the next part of the lesson by saying: **There is One who will stick by us no matter what—God. He will stick by us because He is faithful. Today we will find out more about our faithful God.**

EXPLORATION

Choose one Exploration to help students discover ways God demonstrates His faithfulness in our lives.

EXPLORATION(55-60 minutes)

Materials needed: Bibles, copy of "You Can Count on It" Student Worksheet for each student, pencils, construction paper, magazines, glue, felt pens, scissors.

Step 1: Divide class into pairs. (If necessary, help students find partners.) Give each pair a Bible and have them look up 1 Corinthians 1:9. Ask students to work together to memorize the verse. Then have students change partners. The new pairs test each other on the verse. Ask, **What does it mean that God is faithful? If God says He's going to do something, He will. We can count on Him. Let's find out some ways God is faithful to us.**

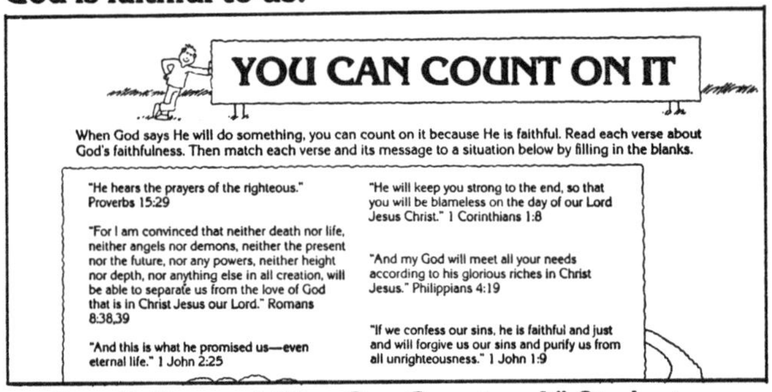
YOU CAN COUNT ON IT

When God says He will do something, you can count on it because He is faithful. Read each verse about God's faithfulness. Then match each verse and its message to a situation below by filling in the blanks.

"He hears the prayers of the righteous." Proverbs 15:29

"For I am convinced that neither death nor life, neither angels nor demons, neither the present nor the future, nor any powers, neither height nor depth, nor anything else in all creation, will be able to separate us from the love of God that is in Christ Jesus our Lord." Romans 8:38,39

"And this is what he promised us—even eternal life." 1 John 2:25

"He will keep you strong to the end, so that you will be blameless on the day of our Lord Jesus Christ." 1 Corinthians 1:8

"And my God will meet all your needs according to his glorious riches in Christ Jesus." Philippians 4:19

"If we confess our sins, he is faithful and just and will forgive us our sins and purify us from all unrighteousness." 1 John 1:9

Step 2: Pass out "You Can Count on It" Student Worksheets, pencils. Have each student work individually to complete the worksheet. When the students are finished ask, **What are some ways God is faithful to us?** Ask students to share examples from the worksheet—and any other ideas they may think of. As each idea is shared ask questions such as: **When have you experienced God's faithfulness in that way? How well do most people seem to understand that idea? What keeps some people from recognizing God's faithfulness?**

Say, **God shows His faithfulness to us in many ways but He does not guarantee that life will always be smooth. He does promise to be with us and help us through whatever circumstances life brings.** Give an example of God's faithfulness in your life during a difficult time. (Examples: God's Word comforted you, friends that helped, physical provisions, inner peace, etc.)

Step 3: Distribute construction paper, magazines, glue, scissors, felt pens. Ask each student to find and cut out the letters of the word faithful. Have each student glue the letters vertically on construction paper and with felt pens create an acrostic (see sketch). Each word or sentence in the acrostic should describe a specific way God has shown His faithfulness in the student's life.

ALTERNATE EXLORATION (50-60 minutes)

Materials needed: Bibles, several sheets of poster board, felt pens, slips of paper lettered with verse references (see *Step 2*), paper, pencils.

Step 1: Same as *Step 1* of original Exploration.

Step 2: Rearrange class into groups of three or four. Give each group a Bible, sheet of poster board and felt pens. Assign each group one or two of the following verses to look up: Proverbs 2:8; Proverbs 15:29; Romans 8:28; 1 Corinthians 1:8; Philippians 4:19; 1 John 1:9; 1 John 2:25. Based on the verse each group read, have each group determine one way God shows His faithfulness to us. Then direct them to illustrate their idea on poster board. Have each group share their poster with the class. Say, **We can count on God's faithfulness, but we can't count on an easy life. It is good to know that whether we go through happy or hard times God's faithfulness to us continues. Can you think of a hard time you (or someone you know) have gone through when God helped in some way? Allow several minutes for volunteers to share.**

Step 3: In the same small groups, have students rephrase their verse to speak directly to a specific problem faced by kids they know. After three or four minutes, ask each group to share their rephrased verses.

Step 4: In groups of three or four, have students create a cheer or rap about the ways God demonstrates His faithfulness to us. The cheerleaders may want to form, with their bodies, the letters of the word faithful saying, "F is for forgiveness, A is for always loving," etc. Have each group present their cheer or rap to the class.

CONCLUSION

Choose a Conclusion activity to help students express thanks to God for specific ways He's been faithful to them.

CONCLUSION (5-7 minutes)

Say, **Sometimes things in our lives become so difficult that we feel as though God has forgotten us. We don't see His faithfulness. When do you think a person might feel that way? During these times it is important to know that God did not cause our suffering but He will prove faithful in helping us through the situation. No matter what we go through we can count on God to be there with us.**

Have each student choose one item on his or her acrostic (from *Step 3* of original Exploration) that he or she would like to thank God for. Lead the students in a prayer time, having volunteers pray sentence prayers. For example, "Thank you, God, for the time we moved and you helped me make new friends." End by saying, **It really pleases God when we notice His faithfulness to us. This week look for ways He demonstrates His faithfulness to you and thank Him for it!**

ALTERNATE CONCLUSION (7-10 minutes)

Materials needed: Pencils, one copy for each student of the "Grateful Graffiti" Student Worksheet.

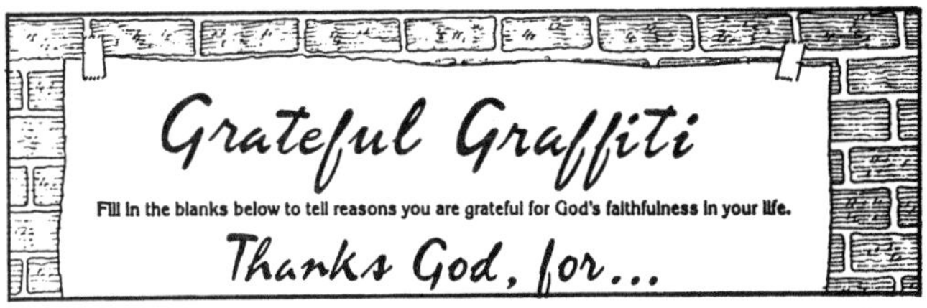

Say, **Sometimes it is difficult to see how God is showing His faithfulness. Can you think of some situations like this?** (Examples: divorce, death, pain, illness.) **During these times we can't always understand God and that's OK, but we can still be confident that He is faithful. If we believe that God is faithful, as it says in 1 Corinthians 1:9, we will begin to see more and more ways that He demonstrates His faithfulness, even in the hard times.**

Direct students to thoughtfully fill in blanks on worksheet. End in prayer, thanking God for the ways He has shown His faithfulness in our lives.

EXTRA FEATURES

Add one or more of these features to your session to increase friendship and impact:

Worship—see page 6.

Games—see page 49.

Munchies—see page 48.

Crafts—see page 50.

God the Judge

KEY VERSE

Nothing in all creation is hidden from God's sight. Everything is uncovered and laid bare before the eyes of him to whom we must give account.
Hebrews 4:13

BIBLICAL BASIS

Psalm 9:8; Matthew 25; Romans 2:5; 3:22-24; 8:1; 1 Corinthians 3:11-15; Ephesians 2:8-10; Hebrews 4:13; 2 Peter 1:10,11

FOCUS OF THE SESSION

God the judge will hold each of us accountable for how we live our lives.

AIMS OF THIS SESSION

During this session each learner will:

- EXAMINE misconceptions people have about God as judge;
- EXPLORE what Jesus taught about judgment day;
- EVALUATE his or her own life and plan a way to be prepared for judgment day.

TEACHER'S BIBLE STUDY

Sterotypes of God

When you picture God on judgment day, what do you think of? Some people see God as the kindly old grandpa in the sky, blind to the faults of people, graciously accepting everyone into His kingdom. Those who see God as the grandfatherly type aren't usually too concerned how they live in this life, thinking it won't really matter to "grandpa" anyway. Typically people with this view of God will not turn to Him in times of need or for strength to live a better life because they see Him as weak and unable to help.

Others see God as a cruel, nitpicking judge who has an itemized list detailing our sins from birth to death. People who see God as the demanding judge often wear themselves out trying to earn enough spiritual brownie points to be accepted by God. Life becomes devoid of joy and peace as a person runs the never-ending treadmill of trying to achieve perfection. Some eventually give up trying and completely turn away from God.

Still others create an image of God fashioned after themselves—the best and most wonderful person they know! A person may think it logical that God is similar to him or herself. Creating God in our own image is convenient because He would then sympathize with and affirm all the choices we make in this life.

Whether we realize it or not, how we view God in His role as judge makes quite an impact on how we live. It is important not to rely on stereotypes or tradition for our view of God but to investigate what the Bible teaches about God as judge. It can be freeing when we realize what He really is like and what He expects from us.

The Parable of the Talents

In Matthew 25:14-30, the parable of the talents, Jesus gives us a picture of Himself as judge. He is represented by a master who, preparing to leave on a journey, calls his servants together. He gives each servant a sum of money (talents) to use, "each according to his own ability." When the master returns he is happy to find the servant who had received five talents has earned five more. The master is equally pleased with the servant who, with two talents, has earned two more. To these two servants the master promises more responsibility and a share in the master's happiness.

The man who had been given one talent has done nothing with it, but has hidden it in the ground because he felt the master was a cruel and unfair man. The master calls him wicked and lazy, takes his talent from him and sends him away forever.

A Just Master

Through this parable we see God (the master) as a judge who has faith in His servants, trusting them with His possessions. He is sensitive, giving them what they can handle and expecting them to be faithful in only that which He has thoughtfully given them to do. We see a judge who on judgment day is eager to build up and reward. Hebrews 6:10 says, *God is not unjust; he will not forget your work and the love you have shown him as you have helped his people and continue to help them.* From the parable we learn that God rewards His faithful servants with more responsibility and shares with them His happiness.

We also see a judge who is discriminating. He is not timid in handing down punishment. To the lazy servant who did nothing with the amount he had been given, the master gives nothing. He takes away the man's one talent and sends him away forever. Romans 2:5 says, *But because of your stubborness and your unrepentant heart, you are storing up wrath against yourself for the day of God's wrath, when his righteous judgment will be revealed.* Those who have had stubborn, unrepentant hearts toward God will be held accountable on the day of judgment.

It is interesting to note the excuse given by the lazy servant—he was afraid because he felt the master was a hard man. This servant held a misconception of what his master was like and based his actions on this misconception. The master held the servant responsible for his view and the resulting actions. So then, we too are responsible to search out an accurate view of God who is true to His Word, and we must then live accordingly.

Day of Judgment

In Acts 17:31 we learn that God has set a day when He will judge the world. Psalm 9:8 tells us that *He will judge the world in righteousness.* Matthew 25:31-46 gives us a picture of Jesus as the judge sitting on His throne in heavenly glory. All nations will be gathered before Him and He will separate the people, sending some to eternal punishment and the righteous to eternal life.

We want to be sure that we are among the righteous on the day of judgment. But who of us can achieve the spotless perfection that is righteousness? Romans 3:22-24 says, *This righteousness from God comes through faith in Jesus Christ to all who believe. There is no difference, for all have sinned and fall short of the glory of God, and are justified freely by his grace through the redemption that came by Christ Jesus.* Ephesians 2:8-10 teaches that our salvation is not a result of works but a gift from God. Good works are the result of our salvation, evidence that we have accepted God's grace and forgiveness. Romans 8:1 says, *Therefore, there is now no condemnation for those who are in Christ Jesus.*

On judgment day God will not expect us to have worked hard enough to achieve righteousness, which is impossible, but He will want to know whether we put our trust in Christ and by faith received the righteousness of God. What was our response to His gospel while we were on earth? Did we care enough to find out who He really is? Did we respond by trusting Him for salvation?

Next God will consider whether we used the "talents" He gave us to make His kingdom grow. In Matthew 25:31-46 those who had trusted in Christ showed it by caring for the sick, the poor and the needy. Those who had humbly served the needs of others were welcomed into the kingdom. Those who had ignored others had in effect ignored Christ and were sent away to eternal punishment.

Paul wrote to the Corinthians, warning that Christians are responsible for what they do with God's blessings. Jesus is the foundation upon which our faith rests, but some build those qualities that last for eternity, while others wastefully give their energies to things that will be destroyed (1 Cor. 3:11-15).

Are You Ready?

We all need to examine our own lives to see if we are prepared for the day of judgment. We do not want to be like the foolish virgins in the parable Jesus told in Matthew 25:1-13. They were not ready when the master came to take them to his banquet. By the time they WERE ready the door was closed and there was no chance of getting in.

We know that we must first trust in Christ as our Savior and Lord and then we must continue to put our trust in Him as we live daily to serve Him. In 2 Peter 1:10 we read, *Therefore, my brothers, be all the more eager to make your calling and election sure. For if you do these things, you will never fall, and you will receive a rich welcome into the eternal kingdom of our Lord and Savior Jesus Christ.* Our foundation of faith in Christ will show itself in the fruit we bear. We bear this fruit only as a result of our being open to God working through us—it is certainly not a result of our own efforts. We not only are solely dependent upon God for our salvation, we also must trust in Him to guide and direct our growth.

As we do "these things" (see 2 Peter 1:10)—growing in Christian character and service—we can be confident that our calling is sure and that we will receive a rich welcome into His heavenly kingdom. We can actually look forward to judgment day. With this in mind, prepare yourself to help those you teach to be ready, out of respect for the righteous judge, knowing that *nothing in all creation is hidden from God's sight. Everything is uncovered and laid bare before the eyes of him to whom we must give account* (Heb. 4:13).

Notes

APPROACH

Choose one Approach activity to introduce your students to the theme of today's session.

APPROACH(5-7 minutes)

Materials needed: Copy for each student of the "What Do You Expect?" Student Worksheet, pencils.

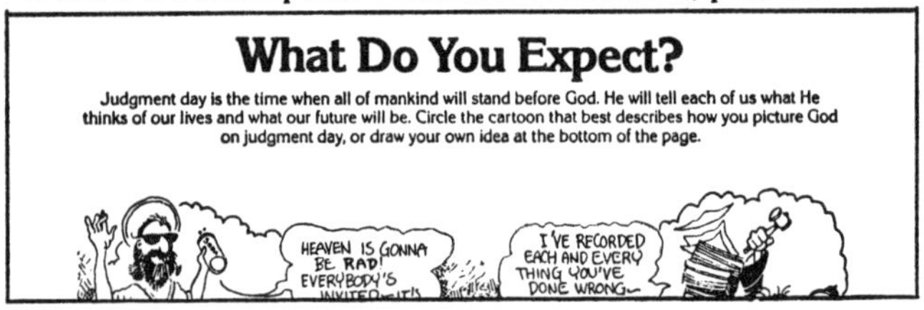
What Do You Expect?

Judgment day is the time when all of mankind will stand before God. He will tell each of us what He thinks of our lives and what our future will be. Circle the cartoon that best describes how you picture God on judgment day, or draw your own idea at the bottom of the page.

Say, **Judgment day is the time when all humanity will stand before God. He will tell each of us what He thinks of our lives and He will decide where each of us will spend eternity.** Have each student read the cartoons on the worksheet and circle the drawing that best depicts what he or she expects on judgment day. If they have an idea other than those shown, they may draw it at the bottom of the page. Allow students to share their answers. Ask, **If Jesus really is like this "cool dude" cartoon how would that affect the way you live? What if God is really a mean old judge? How would you live your life? What if God is a kindly old grandfather who treats us all as innocent children? How would that affect the way you live? Today we are going to find out what kind of judge God is and what we can expect on judgment day.**

ALTERNATE APPROACH(3-5 minutes)

Materials needed: Large sheet of butcher paper, felt pens, tape.

Teacher Preparation: On a large sheet of newsprint draw a picture of a teenager with several empty conversation balloons around him or her. In one of the balloons write, "The devil made me do it." In another write, "But all the kids at school are doing it." Tape the poster to a wall.

Instruct students as they arrrive to fill in the balloons with common excuses they have heard teenagers use for doing something wrong. When everyone has written something say, **All of us at one time or another have given excuses for our behavior and tried to blame our mistakes on others. Sometimes we actually get away with it. But there is a day coming when we'll have to take full responsibility for our actions. We will have to stand before God and no excuse will do as he evaluates our lives. Let's find out what we can expect on judgment day.**

EXPLORATION

Use one of the Exploration suggestions to help students explore what Jesus taught about judgment day.

EXPLORATION(40-50 minutes)

Materials needed: Bibles, copy of "More for Your Money" Student Worksheet for each student, pencils, a cardboard box, a purse and a piggy bank.

Step 1: Pass out Bibles. Ask class to form groups of five. Have students look up Hebrews 4:13 and memorize it by making up actions that go with the verse. Each group should practice together several times and then present their interpretation of the verse to the rest of the group. After the presentations ask, **What does it mean to give an account?** Allow students to respond. Say, **Let's read a rap about a man who made his workers give an account.**

Step 2: Distribute "More for Your Money" Student Worksheets. Have five students volunteer to read in rap-style the various parts of the poem. Allow the three workers to use props (box, purse and piggy bank) to act out their parts. Then discuss the story by asking, **Who were the characters in the story? What were their jobs? How did the workers handle their responsibilities? Do you think Gus was a good boss? Why or why not?**

Step 3: Say, **There is a parable in the Bible much like this story. Jesus told us the parable to help us understand what judgment day would be like. Let's read it now.** Have students turn in their Bibles to Matthew 25:14-30. Direct students to read the passage out loud, each student reading a verse in turn. Ask, **In the parable, whom do the master and servants represent? The master gave each servant talents, or money. What has God given us? What does He expect us to do with what He has given us? Does it matter if we do what God expects? Why? How might people your age "bury" their talents in the ground?**

Step 4: Move class into groups of three students each. Assign each group one or more of these verses to read and report on what it tells about God's judgment—Psalm 9:8; Romans 3:22-24; 1 Corinthians 3:11-15; Ephesians 2:8-10; 2 Peter 1:10,11. Comment and expand where appropriate. Use ideas from the Teacher's Bible Study where needed.

Say, **We learned today that each one of us is responsible for how we live our lives. One day we'll each give an account to God. We don't know exactly when that day will be, so we each need to make sure we are ready. We shouldn't let this idea scare us, but rather it should encourage us to examine our lives and take the steps necessary to be ready for judgment day. Happily, we who trust in Jesus Christ can be sure that God not only counts our faith as righteousness, but also helps us desire to do things that please Him.**

ALTERNATE EXPLORATION(50-60 minutes)

Materials needed: Bibles.

Step 1: Same as *Step 1* in original Exploration.

Step 2: Have class form three groups. Assign each group of students one of the following portions of Scripture to read: Matthew 25:1-13; Matthew 25:14-30; Matthew 25:31-46. Each group must then plan a way to dramatize the Scripture passage, giving the rest of the class an idea of what to expect on judgment day. You may want to provide costumes and props. Allow enough time for groups to plan and rehearse their dramas.

Step 3: After each group presents its parable ask, **Whom did the characters in this parable represent? What does the story teach us about judgment day?**

Step 4: Same as *Step 4* in original Exploration.

CONCLUSION

Choose a Conclusion activity to help students evaluate their lives and prepare themselves for judgment day.

CONCLUSION(10-15 minutes)

Materials needed: Copies of "Here Comes the Judge" Student Worksheet, pencils.

Say, **We've learned there will be a time called judgment day and each one of us will be there. God will judge us according to how we've lived our lives. The most important thing He'll want to know is how we responded to the good news of Jesus. Did we ignore Jesus and live our own way or did we accept Jesus as our Savior and try to live for Him? If you want to be prepared for judgment, you need to ask yourself that question. If you've never asked Jesus to be your Savior and dedicated your life to Him you can do that today. If you are already in God's family, ask yourself, "Am I doing my very best with what He's given me?"**

Pass out "Here Comes the Judge" Student Worksheets. Ask each student to find a quiet spot in the room or outside where he or she can be alone and thoughtfully complete the worksheet. After a few minutes, call the students to come back together. Allow any students who wish to share their "plan of action." Close in prayer.

ALTERNATE CONCLUSION(10-15 minutes)

Materials needed: Large sheets of white paper, pencils, felt pens, crayons, rulers.

Pass out materials. Ask, **How can we be sure that we are prepared for judgment day?** Allow students to respond then say, **When each of us faces God on judgment day, the most important thing will be how we responded to Jesus in our lifetimes. If we made Him the Lord of our lives and earnestly sought to follow Him we do not need to be afraid. God isn't looking for perfect people. He's looking for people who have trusted Christ and have desired to serve Him. Those are the people who will be accepted into His kingdom.**

Instruct each student to create a poster that would help those who read it prepare themselves for judgment day. Display posters around the room. End with a time of prayer in which students can ask for God's help to prepare for judgment day.

Take this opportunity to invite any student who is interested in accepting Christ to talk to you after class.

EXTRA FEATURES:

Add one or more of these features to your session to increase friendship and impact:

Worship—see page 6.
Games—see page 49.
Munchies—see page 48.
Crafts—see page 50.

The Jealous God

KEY VERSE

Do not worship any other god, for the Lord, whose name is Jealous, is a jealous God. Exodus 34:14

BIBLICAL BASIS

Exodus 20:3,4;34:14; Luke 18:18-23; Romans 8:38,39

FOCUS OF THE SESSION

God wants to be number one in the life of each person.

AIMS OF THIS SESSION

During this session each learner will:

- STUDY the story of the rich ruler;
- WRITE things that may compete with God for a believer's attention;
- IDENTIFY what God may be jealous of in his or her life.

TEACHER'S BIBLE STUDY

The First Commandment

Some things cannot be divided. A husband cannot be divided between two women—not without a lot of problems! A loyalty cannot be split between two opposing ideals. And a true Christian cannot be committed to God one minute and to a sinful desire the next.

You and your students will be taking a look at a man whose problem was one of divided commitment. He religiously obeyed the Old Testament laws and commandments in the hope of finding the path to eternal life. Yet when he found the true path—Jesus Christ—he was unable to follow because his money and possessions were more important to him.

Before we take a closer look at Luke 18:18-23—the story of the rich ruler—let's turn back some pages to Exodus 20:2,3. *I am the Lord your God, who brought you out of Egypt, out of the land of slavery. You shall have no other gods before me.*

The very first commandment God carved on the tablets was simple, straightforward, and profound: God first, period. Our devotion is to be to Him. No room is left for division of loyalty or wavering of commitment.

God's claim on our devotion is understandable. After all, He *is* God! He needn't share one bit of credit for His great accomplishments and characteristics. He alone stands eternal. He alone is infinite and perfect. Put another so-called god before Him? Absurd.

The second commandment says in part, *You shall not make for yourself an idol in the form of anything in heaven above or on the earth beneath or in the waters below. You shall not bow down to them or worship them; for I, the Lord your God, am a jealous God* (Ex. 20:4,5). The rest of the commandment speaks of God punishing the children of those who hate Him and rewarding for a thousand generations those who love Him and keep His commandments (see Exod. 20:4-6).

This same stance against division of loyalty is echoed in Exodus 34:14, *Do not worship any other god, for the Lord, whose name is Jealous, is a jealous God.* God is jealous of His position—not jealous in the grasping, hurtful fashion that seems to be connected with human jealousy, but jealous in the loving, protective sense.

God's jealousy is simply His unwillingness to share the devotion of His creatures with any other created thing—be it a god of stone or a hunk of 20th century chrome.

The Rich Ruler

In the New Testament there is probably no better illustration of the Lord's refusal to permit conflicting loyalties than the example of the rich ruler.

In Luke 18:18, the ruler said to Jesus, *Good teacher, what must I do to inherit eternal life?* This may be the most important issue facing humanity: how can we live forever in God's presence? But instead of immediately answering the question, Jesus threw a bit of a curve. *Why do you call me good? No one is good—except God alone* (see v. 19).

This may have been Jesus' way of asking, "Do you really believe I am God?" Christ's comment probably made the man stop and consider. "Good teacher" was a polite title—but did the man really believe it? In the same way, many of your students may address Jesus as Lord or God—but do they really understand the significance of those titles? Does their behavior reflect His Godhood and Lordship in their lives? Part of the joy of being a Christian is becoming more and more like Him as time goes by.

Jesus then told the man, *You know the commandments: "Do not commit adultery, do not murder, do not steal, do not give false testimony, honor your father and mother"* (v. 20). The man answered, *"All these I have kept since I was a boy"* (v. 21).

Here was a completely moral man. This ruler must have shone as a powerful beacon of piety to all around him. If one could reach heaven by proper behavior, then he had nothing to fear. Yet a nagging doubt sent him to Jesus.

Jesus' next statement to the man introduces him to the idea of a jealous God. *You still lack one thing. Sell everything you have and give to the poor, and you will have treasure in heaven. Then come, follow me* (v.22). At this suggestion the battle must have raged in the man's heart, for Jesus had pointed out the one god that the man had put before the true God—the one commandment he had broken. His god was wealth.

Jesus informed him that he could not have both riches and God. As Jesus said in Matthew 6:24: *You cannot serve both God and Money.* One object of desire must go—his pocketbook or eternal life. Tragically, the rich ruler opted to keep the money.

The Jealous God

God demands our undivided loyalty. This demand is based on at least two things: His holiness and His love for us.

Imagine you have invited an acquaintance to dinner. During the meal you realize that person does not want to be there. He doesn't enjoy your company. He's there because you've promised to serve one of your world-famous, history-making chocolate desserts. The person wants the blessings of your lovingly-blended sugar, whipped cream, cocoa and syrup. He's there to gratify his selfish expectation and doesn't really care about you.

This attitude is similar to one that many people have regarding God. They want the eternal life, but following Christ and living by His commands are not a welcome part of the bargain. Because God is holy, He can't allow someone who has fundamentally rejected Him to enjoy the "dessert." Fortunately, God is patient with us. We aren't instantly dropped through the trap door whenever we allow our devotion to wander. God spends a great deal of effort helping us get our priorities right. It can take a long time, but through Bible studies, VBS classes and a myriad of other methods, God can change our hearts.

God's jealousy is also motivated by His love. He knows that it is best for us to sacrifice all and follow Him. After all, He made us—He created us to be His subjects. We cannot be truly fulfilled and complete until we are willingly ruled by Him. He knows that the only way we find lasting joy is when we throw overboard all our baggage, abandon the sinking ship of the world and cling to the spiritual lifesaver with all our might.

Romans 8:38,39 is a wonderful statement about the strength of God's loving jealousy (protectiveness) for us: *For I am convinced that neither death nor life, neither angels nor demons, neither the present nor the future, nor any powers, neither height nor depth, nor anything else in all creation, will be able to separate us from the love of God that is in Christ Jesus our Lord.* Not only does God jealously protect His position as Lord, but He also jealously protects us and our relationship to Him.

Commitment

As you go through this lesson with your students, emphasize the positive aspects of God's loving concern for our welfare. He is jealous of His position as sovereign God not only for His sake, but for ours. He wants to protect our fidelity so that we may indeed be partakers of the eternal life so desperately sought by the rich ruler. Encourage your students to commit themselves to God daily.

Notes

APPROACH

Choose one Approach to introduce your class to the theme of today's lesson.

APPROACH(5-7 minutes)

Materials needed: Copy for each student of the "What's the Word?" Student Worksheet, pencils.

> **What's the Word?**
>
> Your job is to find the word we are looking for. Do this by using your pencil to draw a route from Start to Finish on the maze, collecting letters along the way. When you have finished, unscramble the letters to try and form the word we want. The trouble is, there is more than one path from Start to Finish! It might be

Explain the "What's the Word?" game instructions and be sure everyone understands them. Hand out the worksheets. Give a signal for all to begin. The solution is *jealous.*

When the solution is found, ask students to tell what the word jealous means to them. Ask, **What makes people feel jealous? When was a time that you felt jealous? Do you know that there is something that makes God jealous? There is! It might surprise you to learn that the Bible says God is a jealous God. In what way is He jealous? Let's find out.**

ALTERNATE APPROACH(8-10 minutes)

Materials needed: Several cans of brand-name soda and several cans of its diet version, a small packet of sugar substitute, small paper cups.

Pour students a small amount of each drink and allow them to sample both varieties. Show students both cans of soda. Allow them to see that one can is dietary while the other is the sugared version. Say, **I want you to raise your hand if you think the diet soda tastes best.** (Some students may drink diet sodas as a means of watching their weight—be sure students understand they are not voting for which version they drink most, but which tastes best.) Count the votes and list the number on the chalkboard. **OK, now I want you to raise your hand if you think the regular version is better tasting.** Calculate the winner, which will probably be the regular sugared soda.

Hold up the package of sugar substitute. Say something like, **This is sugar substitute. It's called sugar substitute because it replaces sugar. Our vote indicates that some people prefer the taste of sugar and others prefer the substitute. However, in most areas of life, substitutes never quite match the real thing—whether it's carob in place of chocolate, a second-string quarterback substituting for the star, or a less than wonderful substitute teacher filling in for a favorite teacher. Sometimes we try to find substitutes for God in our lives. Today we will find out how He feels about that and what the results are in our lives.**

EXPLORATION

Use one of the Exploration suggestions to help students learn about putting God first.

EXPLORATION(45-50 minutes)

Materials needed: A copy of "Stiff Competition?" Student Worksheet for every two students, pencils, holepunch, ten index cards, each with a long string attached. Label nine of the cards with one letter each of the letters in "NUMBER ONE." The tenth card is left blank, representing the space between the two words.

Step 1: Write "God is . . . " on the chalkboard (see sketch).

God is __ __ __ __ __ __   __ __ __ .

Hold the index cards in your hand with the strings dangling free. Walk about the room, allowing a different student to grab each of the strings and follow it to the card in your hand. (If you have less than ten students, allow some students to have more than one card.)

When all the cards are distributed, say, **Your job is to fill in the words to the incomplete sentence I've written on the chalkboard. I'm going to ask those of you without cards to help arrange the students holding letters into the correct order to form the two missing words. The blank card represents a space between the two words.** Students with cards move to the front of the room. Others suggest various arrangements, trying different letter combinations until the correct formation is found.

After the words are formed, write them on the chalkboard in the blanks. Say, **The answer is "God is number one." He wants to be first in your life.**

Now I want to read a portion of the Bible to you. Read Exodus 20:1-3.

As you can see, God wants us to have no other gods to replace Him. He wants no substitutes. Now read Exodus 34:14 aloud and say, **The Bible says that God is jealous. Sometimes when humans are jealous it can be a negative thing. We want what others have and are not content with who we are and what we have. Other times human jealousy is well-founded. A child whose parents are too busy with their work, friends or hobbies to spend time with him or her may feel jealous. The child is simply wanting what is rightfully his or hers. When the Bible says that God is jealous it means He wants what is rightfully His—us. He is protective of His place as Lord of our lives.**

Step 2: Have volunteers read Luke 18:18-23. Stop after each verse to ask these questions:

18: How important is the ruler's question? Why?

19: Why do you think Jesus responded with this question and explanation?

20: Why do you think Jesus listed these commandments in answer to the man's question?

21: Assuming the man's claim was true, how would you rate him in comparison to most of the people you know?

22: Why would Jesus ask anyone to do such a thing? Do you think He expects the same of everyone? What other things might Jesus ask other people to give up? Why? Is is fair for God to ask anyone to give up anything?

23: What was the substitute for God in the rich ruler's life? (Wealth.) Do you think he made a wise decision? Why or why not? Is there anything worth substituting for God? Why do so many people seem to be trying to substitute other things for Him?

Step 3: Distribute the "Stiff Competition?" Student Worksheet, one copy to each group of two students. (If a student is left without a partner, you or another leader can do the assignment with him or her.)

Say, **This is a very challenging game. Be sure to draw your pencil lines very lightly. You may want to erase them as you play the game several times in order to improve your score.** Tell students that the purpose of the assignment is to get them thinking about some common things that compete for their devotion to God. Be sure to point out that not all things that compete are bad or evil—but when even good things take the place of God, they become wrong and harmful.

Allow students to play the game for about ten minutes. Calculate who reached the highest score. If you wish, give a reward to the winning team. Lead a detailed discussion of the things that compete with God—those listed on the game and any that the students thought of themselves. Ask, **How can you decide if an activity is competing with God in your life? If you sense an activity has taken God's place in your life, what steps should you take? If the ruler who came to Jesus had let (TV) become a substitute for God, what would Jesus have said to him?**

Say, **God wants to be Lord of your life because He loves you. He wants to protect and guide you. He knows that putting your trust in money, popularity or intelligence will only lead to hurt and disappointment.**

ALTERNATE EXPLORATION (50-60 minutes)

Materials needed: A copy for each pair of students of the "Stiff Competition?" Student Worksheet, pencils, dark glasses.

Step 1: Wear the dark glasses. Ask your students, **Besides making me look like a movie star, what purpose do these glasses serve?** (The glasses protect your eyes from the sun.)

Now I want to read three verses from the Bible to you. Read Exodus 20:1-3.

As you can see, God wants us to have no other gods to replace Him. He wants no substitutes. Now read Exodus 34:14 and say, **The Bible says that God is jealous.**

Point out to your students that God's jealous desire to be number one in each person's life is really for our own protection. **Without the protection of dark glasses, your eyes could be burned and damaged. Similarly, staying close to God is our protection. If we stray away from Him, we also will be burned and hurt.**

God wants to be number one not only because He deserves to be, but because it is the very best thing that could happen to us.

Step 2: Same as *Step 2* in the original Exploration.

Step 3: Same as *Step 3* in the original Exploration.

Step 4: Have class form groups of four or five. Instruct each group to come up with a commercial to "get the word out" that God is a jealous God. The commercial should also instruct its viewers as to what our response to God's jealousy should be. Have each group present its commercial to the class.

CONCLUSION

Use one of the Conclusions to help each student identify a person or thing that God may be jealous of in his or her life.

CONCLUSION (5-7 minutes)

Materials needed: Copies of the "Reason to Be Jealous" Student Worksheet, pencils.

Have students work individually to complete the "Reason to Be Jealous" Student Worksheet. End in prayer, asking God to help everybody put Him first in their lives each day.

ALTERNATE CONCLUSION (7-10 minutes)

Materials needed: Bibles, pencils and index cards.

Pass out Bibles, pencils and index cards. Instruct students to look on their "Stiff Competition?" Student Worksheet and circle one thing that God may be jealous of in their lives. Say, **It is possible for God to be number one in our lives. Take some time right now to talk to God about the thing you circled. Ask for his help in putting Him first.** Allow a few minutes for students to talk to God silently.

Next, have students look up Exodus 34:14 and write the verse on an index card. Have them work in pairs to memorize the verse. Say, **Whenever you notice that something is becoming more important to you than God, repeat the verse to yourself and ask for God's help. Keep the card in a place where you will see it often.** Invite students to join you in prayer as you ask God for help in putting Him first. Invite those who wish to talk with you to stay after class.

EXTRA FEATURES

Add one or more of these features to your session to increase friendship and impact:

Worship—see page 6.
Games—see page 49.
Munchies—see page 48.
Crafts—see page 50.

The Incomprehensible God

KEY VERSE
How awesome is the Lord Most High, the great King over all the earth! Psalm 47:2

BIBLICAL BASIS
Psalm 139:3,4;145:3; Isaiah 40:12-31;44:6;55:8,9; Jeremiah 23:24; John 1:1

FOCUS OF THE SESSION
God's greatness is beyond our imagination; He is worthy of our awe and respect.

AIMS OF THIS SESSION
During this session each learner will:
- LIST several attributes of God;
- DESCRIBE how the greatness of God affects him or her personally;
- HAVE AN OPPORTUNITY to praise God for His greatness.

TEACHER'S BIBLE STUDY

The Incomprehensible God

Contemplating God and what He is like can overwhelm the mind more than any other pursuit of human thought. It can cause our thoughts to hit a dead end. Pondering God's power, perfect knowledge, justice and holiness can be stimulating and enlightening, but we may soon feel the need to return to thinking about attributes of God that are more easily comprehended.

Trying to take in thoughts too big to comprehend often leads to frustration. This uncomfortable feeling leads us to the recognition that there are aspects of God that are awesome and mysterious. These aspects are far removed from the familiar human images of Father and Comforter and they place God in the realm of the uncharted. As we try to focus, the only thing that begins to be clear to us is that God is truly incomprehensible to our limited thinking.

The idea of a God who works according to a timetable or in a logical manner is comforting to humans. We are secure with a system that is intellectually understandable. To be sure, there is much about God that we *can* comprehend. But there is a side of Him that is far beyond our comprehension.

Great Is the Lord

Some of the scientific theories developed by human beings are mind-boggling. For example, comprehending all of Einstein's theory of relativity is impossible for most people. Just think, if man's theories can be so complex yet only touch the fringes of God's thoughts, then God must be much further beyond our comprehension. After all, His nature transcends our whole sphere of existence.

A measure of God's greatness can be glimpsed in His handiwork. People often point to the beauty of nature as a reflection of God's creativity and love. By studying the complexity of the world around us we can learn to appreciate God's intricate and bewildering creativity. Recent scientific findings help make it clear that God is the Creator of some staggering phenomena.

One example: It is estimated that a round-trip voyage to the nearest galaxy, Andromeda, would take at least 140,000 years traveling at the speed of light (approximately 186,000 miles per second). That means by the time the space ship left earth and returned, the earth would have aged fantastically. But the voyagers who made this trip at the speed of light would have grown older by only about 30 years.

Modern science may reinforce the idea that God is far more complex than we can imagine, but ancients knew this as well. Their awe is recorded in the pages of both the New and Old Testament Scriptures.

The God Who Surrounds Us

The Bible records the idea that God is inescapable: He surrounds us completely. He controls time and He encompasses eternity. Since God is infinite and eternal, He can dwell in the distant past as well as the distant future. Time cannot limit Him. With God everything is now. He knows our past and our future. The psalmist says, *You discern my going out and my lying down; you are familiar with all my ways. Before a word is on my tongue you know it completely, O Lord* (Ps. 139:3,4).

Time exerts no power over God. When time began, God was there (see Gen. 1:1; Eccles. 3:11). He surrounds it. He holds it in His hand and is not bound by time's dictates.

The Unsearchable God

Another idea that the Scripture teaches about God is that we cannot hope to figure out everything about Him. He defies adequate description. The psalmist again writes *His greatness no one can fathom* (Ps. 145:3). The apostle Paul declares in his doxology: *Oh, the depth of the riches of the wisdom and knowledge of God! How unsearchable his judgments and his paths beyond tracing out!* (Rom. 11:33).

We can only know God because He has created within us the capacity to know Him. But we can know of God only what He has revealed to us and what He has given us insight to understand.

The Bible makes it quite clear that sinful humanity and God do not think alike. *For my thoughts are not your thoughts, neither are your ways my ways, declares the Lord* (Isa. 55:8). *No one knows the thoughts of God except the Spirit of God* (1 Cor. 2:11b).

Although many of us realize that God's ways are far beyond our understanding, we generally search for concrete reasons why things happen to us. Instead of resting in God's wisdom, we may struggle to understand our circumstances and impatiently create our own solutions. Perhaps your students have subconsciously learned from television that complex problems can be solved in 30 to 60 minutes. They have come to expect immediate, simple solutions. Waiting for God's timing is a difficult concept, but an important one to reinforce to your students.

He Was and Is and Is to Come

Another perplexing concept the Bible teaches is that God is self-existent—that is, He has no creator Himself. Of course we cannot fathom such a thing. Everything that we know has an origin. Every child has parents. How could God just exist? John 1:1 says that in the beginning the Word already existed. While most of us accept the idea that God has always existed, to actually THINK about it leads us straight into an impossible, baffling maze that we quickly want to exit.

Awe-Inspiring Majesty

However, thinking about an incomprehensible God is not mere mind-play. It is not a spiritual Rubik's cube. It serves a practical purpose. First, it should give us a sense of awe. We cannot help but be humbled by the tremendous Lord we serve who not only stretches our imagination but stumps it as well.

A healthy case of awe usually leads to a humble, more realistic view of ourselves. We can see that we are not so spectacular and self-dependent. We are creations, not gods.

A view of God's majesty should also lead to obedience. We can come to the point where we realize that God is much smarter than we are and it would simply be best to obey Him. When we have made up our minds to obey God we are sometimes stretched beyond our limits of understanding. The result is that our faith increases. The next step is that the cycle continues and obedience and faith feed off each other for mutual benefit. It then becomes a matter of life-style to obey God whether or not we understand the reason why.

The fraction of God that we can comprehend is more than most of us can cope with. We still see "but a poor reflection" but someday He will stretch us beyond our imaginations to see Him "face to face" (see 1 Cor. 13:12). Until that time we can fall down and worship Him because of His greatness. We can join the psalmist who declared, *I will exalt you, my God the King; I will praise your name for ever and ever. Every day I will praise you and extol your name for ever and ever. Great is the Lord and most worthy of praise; His greatness no one can fathom.* (Ps. 145:1-3).

Notes

THIS WEEK'S TEACHING PLAN

APPROACH

Select an Approach to help stretch your students' view of God.

APPROACH(5-7 minutes)

Materials needed: Two large pictures (from a magazine, poster, etc.), a sheet of construction paper to cover each picture, scissors, tape.

Cut a small hole in each sheet of construction paper, then place one sheet over each picture. Use tape to attach the sheet of paper along the top edge of the picture. Post the covered pictures at the front of the class. Ask students to guess what each picture looks like by looking at the small portion revealed by the hole. Remove the covers so students can see how they did. Move to the Exploration by saying: **The little bit of the pictures we saw gave us an idea about the whole, but the picture had much more in it than we realized at first. Often our view of God is like that. We know only a little about Him, and He is much greater, wiser and more powerful than we imagine. We will try to expand our view of God in today's lesson.**

ALTERNATE APPROACH(7-10 minutes)

Materials needed: Copy for each student of the "From This Angle" Student Worksheet, pencils.

Ask students to read the "From This Angle" cartoon and then create their own blind man dilemma cartoon in the space below. Allow several minutes for the students to work, then invite volunteers to share their cartoons. Ask, **What do you see as the point of these cartoons?** (It's easy to jump to wrong conclusions with only partial information.) Make a transition to the next part of the lesson by saying: **Each of the blind men knew something about the elephant but none of them had the whole picture. People try to figure out God by looking at only parts of His nature. What they know about God may be right but their concept is too limited by not realizing there is much about God beyond our human abilities to understand. Today we want to stretch and expand our thinking about God so that we have a better idea of what He is like.**

EXPLORATION

Use one of the Exploration suggestions to help your students discover some of the great and powerful aspects of God's character.

EXPLORATION(60 minutes)

Materials needed: Copy for each student of "Beyond Description" Student Worksheet, pencils, paper, dictionary, chalkboard and chalk.

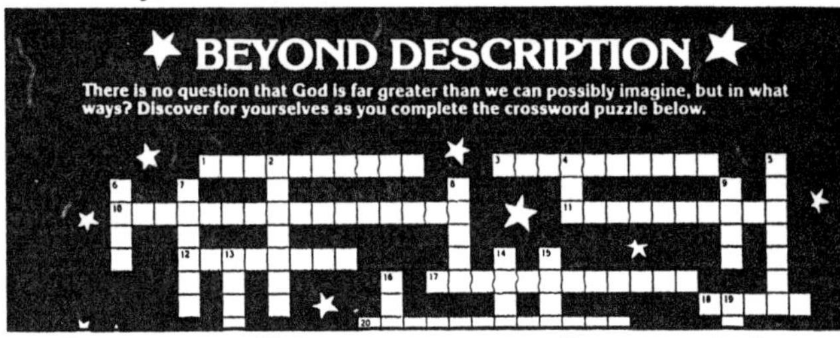

Preparation: Make arrangements for a panel of pastors, elders, etc., to be guests during *Step 3* of the Exploration. They will be answering students' questions about God.

Step 1: On the chalkboard, write: God is __________. Have students take turns guessing letters that might be in the 16-letter mystery word. When a student guesses a letter correctly write the letter in the correct space(s) and give that student another turn. See who can be the first to guess "incomprehensible." Ask if anyone knows what incomprehensible means. Have one student look it up in the dictionary and read the definition to the class. Say, **Today we'll find out just how incomprehensible God is.**

Step 2: Divide class into groups of two. Distribute "Beyond Description" Student Worksheet and pencils. Have pairs work together to complete the crossword puzzle.

Step 3: Ask each pair to choose the most interesting thing they learned about God from the crossword puzzle and plan a way to pantomime it in front of the class. They may do any action but may not speak. As each attribute is guessed by the class, write it on the chalkboard and ask, **Why is it important for us to know this about God?** After all attributes about God have been shared, ask, **Which attribute of God do you think is hardest for most people to accept? Why?**

Step 4: Distribute sheets of paper. Instruct students to think of some difficult questions they might have about God. Allow ten minutes for students to think, and then write down their questions. Bring in the guest panel and have students ask their questions. The panel won't have all the answers, so encourage panel members to tell students how they deal with not understanding everything about our great God.

After panel discussion, ask, **What difference can the realization of God's greatness make in our lives?**

ALTERNATE EXPLORATION(50-60 minutes)

Materials needed: Bibles, poster board, felt pens, manila envelopes, pencils, paper, scissors, chalkboard and chalk or overhead transparency and projector.

Preparation: To prepare for *Step 2,* look up each of the following Scripture passages and letter each on a separate slip of paper: Psalm 139:3,4; Isaiah 40:21,22; Isaiah 40:25,26; Isaiah 55:8,9; John 1:1; Romans 11:33-36.

Step 1: Pass out Bibles and pencils. Ask students the following questions and have them write down their answers: **What is the largest thing you have ever seen? Who is the strongest person you have ever seen? What is the most powerful thing you have ever seen? Who is the wisest person you've ever met? What is the most beautiful sight you've ever seen?** Allow students to share their answers. Say, **All of us have seen some of the amazing things God has created. We've seen or known some amazing people, but the greatest people or things are nothing compared to God.** Direct students to turn to Isaiah 40:12-17 in their Bibles. Allow them to take turns reading the verses out loud. Say, **God is so great and powerful that He is beyond our understanding—He is incomprehensible.**

Step 2: Divide your class into groups of three to five. Distribute a slip of paper with a Scripture passage written on it, scissors, felt pens, poster board and a manila envelope to each group. Instruct each group to read their passage and then illustrate it by creating a picture puzzle. Have the students draw their picture on poster board and then cut it up into puzzle pieces. You may want to tell your students how many pieces to cut. Instruct the students to put the cut-up pieces in a manila envelope and then deliver it to another group who will put the puzzle together. You may wish to make this a contest, awarding a prize to the first group to correctly assemble a puzzle.

Have students share the various attributes of God they illustrated and record them on the chalkboard or overhead transparency.

Step 3: Same as *Step 4* of the original Exploration.

CONCLUSION

Choose a Conclusion activity to help students express praise to God.

CONCLUSION(7-10 minutes)

Materials needed: Small slips of paper, pencils.

Ask the students to look at the list of attributes compiled during the Exploration and choose the one that means the most to them. Allow students to share which attribute they chose and why.

Then say, **The Bible says that since God is so great He deserves our praise.** Read Psalm 48:1a to the class, then pass out slips of paper and pencils. Ask each student to write down one thing he or she wants to praise God for. Letter the words to Psalm 47:2 on the chalkboard. Lead the students in a praise litany. The first student begins by saying, "I praise God because ... " then the class recites Psalm 47:2. Repeat this procedure until all the students have had a chance to express their praise to God. End by singing a short praise song.

ALTERNATE CONCLUSION(10-15 minutes)

Materials needed: Paper, pencils.

Ask the students to look at the list of attributes compiled during the Exploration and choose the one that means the most to them. Allow students to share which attribute they chose and why.

Divide class into groups of three or four. Ask each group to write a short poem to God about His greatness. When students have completed their poems, begin a praise litany by having one of the students read Psalm 47:2. Then have a volunteer from each group share their poem. Conclude by praying together.

EXTRA FEATURES

Add one or more of these features to your session to increase friendship and impact:

Worship—see page 6.
Games—see page 49.
Munchies—see page 48.
Crafts—see page 50.

Munchies

Each day vary the refreshments you provide. The following nutritional and "not-so-nutritional" refreshment suggestions go beyond the usual punch and cookies. The suggestions marked with a star ★ can be prepared by the students during snack time. NOTE: If you have students who cannot eat sweets, make sure to bring an alternate snack for them.

1. *Safari Bars*—1 cup peanut butter, 1 cup nuts, 1 cup raisins, 1 cup toasted wheat germ, 1 cup shredded coconut, 1 cup or more (add until mixture is not sticky) granola cereal. Mix all ingredients and press into pan or form into small bars. (Serves 10-15.)

2. *Pizza Rounds*—Spread halves of English muffins with pizza sauce. Sprinkle with parmesan cheese and bake in a 350 degree (177 degrees Celsius) oven for 5-10 minutes until warm and bubbly.

★ 3. *Snack on a Spear*—Have your students spear nibbles such as cubes of cheese, meat or fruit on straight pretzels. They become much more fun to eat this way.

4. *Tarantula Treats*—1 cup chocolate pieces, 1/4 cup peanut butter, 1 5-oz. can chow mein noodles, 1/2 cup apple juice concentrate, 1 teaspoon vanilla. Melt and stir together the first four ingredients in the top of a double boiler. Add noodles. Stir carefully, breaking up noodles as you gradually coat them with the chocolate mixture. Drop by spoonfuls onto a cookie sheet that has been covered with waxed paper. Let treats harden in the refrigerator.

★ 5. *Trail Mix*—Mix peanuts, raisins, sunflower seeds, M and M's and Reese's Pieces in a large bowl.

★ 6. *Jungle Cooler*—1 cup cantaloupe chunks, 1 cup sliced bananas, 1/2 cup apple juice concentrate, 1 cup milk. Mix ingredients together in a blender for a sweet, foamy drink. Makes eight 4-oz. servings.

7. *Outback Bites*—1 (6-oz.) package butterscotch pieces, 1/3 cup peanut butter, 2 tablespoons butter, 3 cups miniature marshmallows, 1/4 teaspoon salt, 2 1/2 quarts popped corn, 1 cup granola, 1 (6-oz.) package semi-sweet chocolate pieces. Melt butterscotch pieces, peanut butter, butter, marshmallows and salt in top of double boiler over hot water. Stir until smooth. Add mixture to popped corn and granola in buttered 9 × 13-inch pan. Toss until mixed. Press into pan. Melt chocolate in double boiler, then spread over mixture. Cool until firm. Cut into bars.

★ 8. *Hikers' Handy Snack*—Core apples and fill them with soft cheese or peanut butter.

★ 9. *Purple Parrot Shake*—1/4 cup grape juice, 1 cup milk, 1 sliced banana. Mix all ingredients in a blender. Makes two servings.

10. *Tropical Treat*—2 cups canned or fresh pineapple chunks, 2 cups sliced peaches, 1 cup concentrated apple juice (thawed), 1 teaspoon cinnamon, 1 1/2 tablespoons quick-cooking tapioca, 1/2 cup whole-wheat flour, 1/4 cup butter or margarine, 1/2 cup rolled oats. In large bowl, combine first five ingredients. Mix well; pour into 8 × 8-inch baking dish. In separate bowl, combine flour and butter; mix with a fork until crumbly. Mix in oats. Sprinkle the flour-oats mixture over fruit. Bake at 375 degrees for 30 minutes.

11. *Jungle Goo*—3 cups sugar, 1/3 cup cocoa, 3/4 cup milk. Boil and stir for 8 minutes, then add 1 stick margarine and 1 teaspoon vanilla. Cool until sticky. Stir one or all of the following into the goo: Rice Krispies, Cheerios, raisins, coconut, nuts, marshmallows, peanut butter, oatmeal. With wet hands, mold the treats into balls, lollipops or flat shapes. Place on waxed paper until cool.

★ 12. *Celery Logs*—Try a new stuffing for celery. Have students mix equal portions of grated carrots, peanut butter and spoon-size shredded wheat (smashed or grated). Press mixture into celery sticks.

★ 13. *Pretzel Ropes*—1 package yeast, 1 1/2 cups warm water, (105-115 degrees), 1/2 teaspoon sugar, 4 1/2 cups flour, 1 egg yolk, 2 tablespoons water, coarse salt, sesame seeds. Dissolve yeast in warm water and add sugar. Add flour and knead 6 minutes. Let dough rise, covered, in a greased bowl until double in size. Divide the dough into 12 pieces and let your students roll and twist into ropes. Blend together the egg and the water and have students brush some of the mixture onto their pretzels. Next let them sprinkle on some coarse salt or sesame seeds. Students place their pretzels on a cookie sheet. Bake at 450° for 12 minutes.

★ 14. *Sandwich Boat*—Hollow out hot dog buns. Let students fill their Sandwich Boats with egg salad, chicken salad or ham salad.

Games

Hikers' Helpers

Materials: Large lace-up hiking boots.

Procedure: Divide class into pairs and give each pair one hiking boot. At a given signal, one member of each pair must take off his or her shoe and put on the boot. The pair then works together to lace up the boot, using only one hand each. When the boot is laced, the person wearing it must hop to a designated location, using only the foot in the boot. The partner may help. The first pair to reach the designated spot wins.

Sailboat Race

Materials: String, several waxed paper cups, scissors.

Procedure: Divide class into two or more teams. Have each team stand in a straight line. Give each team a length of string that will reach the length of the line. Have the first and the last player in each line hold an end of their string. Give the first player in each line a waxed paper cup with a hole in the bottom. That player threads the cup onto the string and then pulls the string taut. When the leader says "go," the first team member blows the cup until it reaches the second person, who blows until it reaches the third person, and so on. The first team to blow the sailboat to the end of its line wins.

Balloon Volleyball

Materials: Several large balloons, string or masking tape.

Procedure: Divide classroom down the middle by placing a line of string or masking tape on the floor. Inflate several balloons. Divide the class into two teams and have teams sit on either side of the tape, facing one another in rows as in regular volleyball. The balloon should be served from the front row. Use the same rules as in regular volleyball, except players must remain seated as they hit the balloon back and forth over the line.

Lion's Mouth

Materials: Heavy red cloth, cut into a 5-foot (1.5-m) circle.

Procedure: Place the cloth circle on the floor or ground in the center of a large playing area. Divide group into four teams of equal size. Have teams stand facing each other around the cloth circle. (The circle represents the lion's mouth.) Have players grasp each others' wrists and enlarge the circle. When the teacher says "go" each team tries to pull the members of the other teams into the lion's mouth. A player who touches the lion's mouth with any part of his or her body is out and must leave the circle. Any player who lets go of another player's wrist is also out. After a player steps out, the players remaining join wrists and resume play. The team having the greatest number of players still in the game after a three- to five-minute period is the winner.

Quick Draw

Materials: Two large newsprint pads, two felt pens, several slips of paper.

Teacher Preparation: Place a table and chairs at each end of the room. Write a different noun or verb on each slip of paper.

Procedure: Divide class into two teams. Have each team sit around a table. Provide each team with a pad of newsprint and a felt pen. Each team sends a representative to the teacher who is in the middle of the room. The teacher shows the representatives a slip of paper with a word written on it. They must run back to their teams and attempt to illustrate that word. They must not talk, or write any words. The first team to correctly guess the word gets 100 points. Repeat this procedure using different representatives and words until everyone has had a turn. The winning team is the one with the most points at the end of the game.

Mailman Hold-Up

Materials: Envelopes with names of cities, states, or countries lettered on them, blindfold.

Procedure: Have the group form a large circle with chairs. Have a volunteer "bandit" stand in the center of the circle wearing a blindfold. Give each seated player an envelope with the name of a city or country written on it.

The teacher then announces that a letter is being sent from "Hawaii" to "Alaska." Whoever is holding these envelopes must exchange letters and seats and try to escape being "held up" by the blindfolded bandit. The bandit tries to grab a letter, and if successful, he or she may remove the blindfold and take a place in the circle. The player who lost his or her letter dons the blindfold and the game continues as the teacher announces the next letter to be sent.

Safari Scrunch

Procedure: Ask for a volunteer to be the "safari leader." The volunteer hides somewhere within the boundaries defined by the teacher. (The boundaries could include several rooms, a whole building or an outside yard area.) The rest of the group counts to fifty and then each player goes his or her own way to search for the "lost" safari leader. Upon finding the safari leader, the searcher quickly hides with him or her, trying not to alert other searchers. The next searcher who comes upon the hiders quietly joins them and the hiding group grows until often they are scrunched into a very small space. When the last member of the group discovers the hiders, the game begins again with a new safari leader.

Elbow Link Tag

Procedure: Divide group into pairs. Have members of each pair link their elbows, placing hands on their waists. Pairs stand at a distance from each other to fill playing area. One player volunteers to be "it," another volunteers to be the runner. When the leader says, "go" the "it" chases the runner, attempting to tag him or her. The runner can avoid being tagged by linking elbows with a member of any pair standing nearby. Immediately, the member of the pair on the other end must unlink elbows and become the runner. When the runner is tagged, he or she becomes "it," and the previous "it" becomes the runner.

Twister

Procedure: This is a variation of the familiar commercial game. The teacher simply calls out various parts of the body that must then be connected to objects in the room. For example, the leader may call, "head to wall, toe to table, elbow to floor." As instructions are added it becomes more difficult for players to keep their balance. The last player standing is the winner of the game.

Sock It to 'Em

Materials: Several old sheets or blankets.

Procedure: Cover a large, grassy playing area with the sheets or blankets. All players must take off their shoes, but leave their socks on. When teacher says "go," players crawl around playing area attempting to remove each other's socks. No one may stand up or kick another player. When a person has lost both socks, he or she is eliminated. The last player with a sock on is the winner.

Craft Projects for Youth Groups

"Oh sure! Craft projects for my youth group. They'd sooner swim with alligators! *I'd* sooner swim with alligators!"

WAIT! Don't turn the page yet! We have actually had reports from some youth workers that craft projects were a BIG HIT with their young people. (These youth leaders aren't quite ready to release their names for publication. Social stigma and all that . . . you understand.)

Anyway, these leaders found the following to be true:

1. Young people will groan and roll their eyes heavenward when told, "We're going to make a craft now."
2. To keep the respect of your youth group, never say the word craft. That word is the ultimate no-no.
3. It is possible for your youth group to "do crafts" and enjoy it—without the word craft ever being mentioned. Simply say something like this: "I'm ready for a little change of pace. Let's move into the rec room" (or over to the art tables, or wherever) "and try our hands at a little creative mischief."

   This creative break need not be a break from the focus of the session. It's a great time for you, the youth worker, to model concepts that have just been studied. It's also an excellent time to have casual conversation about the application of the concepts.
4. The end result (finished product) isn't nearly as important as the process of being creative and having a good time with each other.

During this time of informal interaction, the youth can develop new friendships and strengthen existing friendships. It's also within this informal context that you can get a better look at the personalities of your young people. Your ministry effectiveness will be enhanced as you become more aware of the individual spiritual and emotional needs of those in your youth group.

So don't be appalled at the mere thought of embarking upon "craft projects" with those wild and woolly youth the Lord has temporarily put in your hands. Why don't you try some of this creative diversion and see for yourself. The possibilities for projects are limitless. You may want to use some of the suggestions in the Youth section of *Trunkful of Crafts.*

Student Worksheets

The following pages contain the

Student Worksheets

for this course.

For complete instructions, please read page 5.

A HELPFUL NOTE:
It is NOT necessary for you to reproduce every Student Worksheet for each session!

- We have provided many pages as alternatives. Choose only the ones you intend to use in class.
- Some worksheets contain only a sentence or two of information or a portion of Scripture. This has been included for your convenience, primarily for making overhead projector transparencies. You can avoid copying these by handing out blank paper to your students and simply **reading** the instructions aloud or writing them on the chalkboard. Or, in the case of Scripture sections, make overhead projector transparencies for the class to read. (**WARNING:** Be sure to use the kind of transparency designed for use in copiers. If the copier jams, ordinary acetate plastic melts inside a hot copier!)
- The editors of *Getting to Know Our Awesome God* recognize that too much of a good thing—even Student Worksheets—can be too much. Seek variety in your teaching times. Spice up your classes with a guest speaker, or show a good Christian film for discussion. Even a trip to the donut shop can give you an opportunity to disciple your students!

What Do You Call Your Parents?

Which of the following names do you use when addressing your dad or mom?
Circle the ones that you use most often.
Put a **square** around ones that, if you said them, would get you killed.
Put a **triangle** around terms that, if you used them, would get you a weird look.

PA/MA

HEY YOU

DAD/MOM

MASTER/MISTRESS

______________________ (write your own here)

SENOR/SENORA

OLD MAN/OLD LADY

POP/MUM

THE MAN/THE WOMAN

DADDY/MOMMY

FATHER/MOTHER

SIR/MA'AM

GENERAL

POPPA/MAMA

POPS/MOMS

PATER/MATER

PAPPY/MAMMY

THE IDEAL FATHER

Match each verse below to the phrase on the right that describes it.

"O Lord, you have searched me and you know me." Psalm 139:1

"The Lord watches over all who love him." Psalm 145:20a

"The Lord takes delight in His people." Psalm 149:4

"For God so loved the world that he gave his one and only Son, that whoever believes in him shall not perish but have eternal life." John 3:16

Jesus said, "Anyone who has seen me has seen the Father." John 14:9

"We have different gifts according to the grace given us." Romans 12:6

"So do not worry, saying, 'What shall we eat?' or 'What shall we drink?' or 'What shall we wear?' For the pagans run after all these things, and your heavenly Father knows that you need them. But seek first his kingdom and his righteousness, and all these things will be given to you as well." Matthew 6:31-33

"Call to me and I will answer you and tell you great and unsearchable things you do not know." Jeremiah 33:3

"But the Counselor, the Holy Spirit, whom the Father will send in my name, will teach you all things and will remind you of everything I have said to you." John 14:26

"God is our refuge and strength, an ever present help in trouble." Psalm 46:1

- God is a Father who teaches His children.
- God is a Father who takes the time to know His kids.
- God is a Father who wants us to know Him so He sent His Son, Jesus, to show us what He is like.
- God is a Father who is always looking out for His children.
- God is a Father who responds to His children when they call to Him.
- God is a Father who gives His children a life with Him forever.
- God is a Father who gives gifts to His children.
- God is a Father who provides food, drink and clothes for His children.
- God is a Father who enjoys His children.
- God is a Father who is strong enough to help His children with their problems.

Circle your favorite thing about God the Father.
Why is this your favorite?

Imagine that God wants to advertise the fact that He is looking for children to adopt into His family. He has decided to place a want ad in the newspaper. In the space below, write what might appear in God's want ad. Make sure to include:

- What He has to offer those who want to be in His family.
- The way that a person becomes a member of His family.
- How to contact God.

Junior Come HOME
THE STORY OF THE PRODIGAL SON RETOLD
(SEE LUKE 15: 11-32 FOR THE ORIGINAL UNCUT VERSION.)
HEY, POP! I WANT MY BUCKS NOW!
HUH?
I DON'T WANNA WAIT 'TIL I'M OLD AND MOLDY TO HAVE FUN. I WANNA HAVE IT NOW!
THAT'S AGAINST MY BETTER JUDGMENT, SON.
COME ON, DAD! I WON'T BLOW IT! I'VE GOT A GREAT LEAD ON SOME FOREIGN INVESTMENTS!
SO...
STILL AGAINST MY BETTER JUDGMENT...
SNIFF
BYE, FOLKS!
STUPID LITTLE BROTHER!
FAR, FAR AWAY—
HOIST ANOTHER ONE, MATE!
AFTER ALL, IT'S YOUR PARTNERSHIP* THAT'S PAYING FOR IT!
THUD!
* THE "PARTNERSHIP"—HE PAYS, THEY DRINK
BUT I'M OUTA MONEY.
THEN YOU'RE OUTA HERE!
WACK!
DESTITUTE, THE KID COMPETES WITH PIGS FOR FOOD!
DIBS
UNTIL ONE DAY—
YOU KNOW...I'D BE A LOT BETTER OFF AS A LOW PAID SERVANT BACK ON DAD'S RANCH. AT LEAST I COULD EAT!
AND SO—
DAD, I REALLY BLEW IT! I'M NOT WORTHY TO BE YOUR SON! IS THERE ANY CHANCE I COULD GET A JOB AS A PEON?
PHEW! WELL, SON—I'LL NOT ONLY FORGIVE YOU BUT WELCOME YOU BACK INTO OUR FAMILY! BUT NO MORE FOREIGN INVESTMENTS! NOW GET A BATH!
TOM FINLEY

The Shredded Sheet

Find how the shredded pieces of this letter fit together to form two Bible verses. Write the verses in the pencils below. Check your answers by looking them up in the Bible. Circle any words or phrases that describe God's will for us. Then finish the letter by writing what you might say to someone who is following his or her own path away from God, the Father.

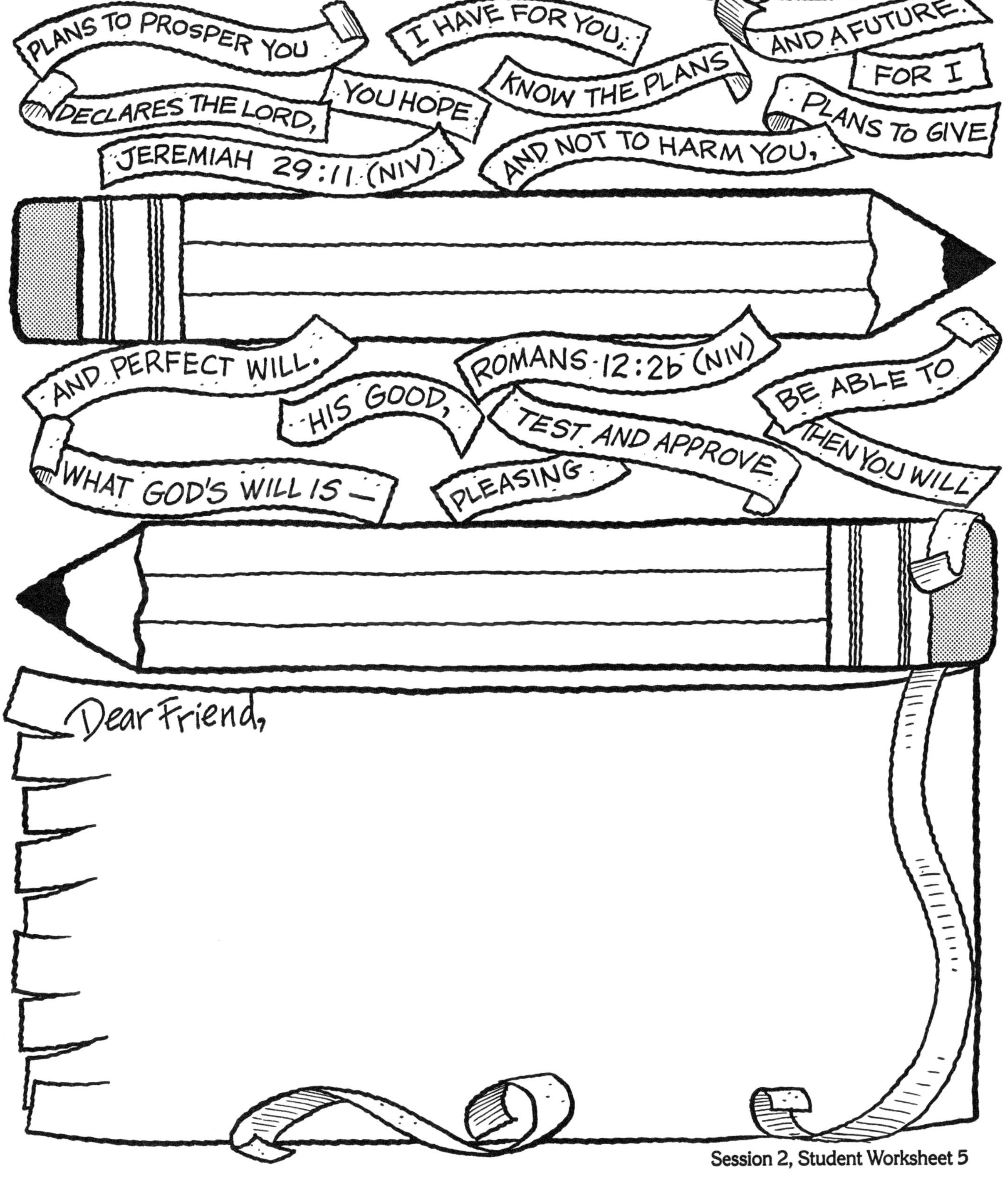

Take My Advice, Kid

In the following blanks write what you think MIGHT happen in each situation . . .
(There are no right or wrong answers.)

If Sue follows her dad's rules . . .

If Sue does not follow her dad's rules . . .

POSTCARD

If Andy follows his mom's advice . . .

If Andy does not follow his mom's advice . . .

POSTCARD

POSTCARD

If Michael obeys his father . . .

If Michael does not obey his father . . .

POSTCARD

If Kim follows her mom's instructions . . .

If Kim does not follow her mom's instructions . . .

THE LOST SON GAME

Cut out the cards below and on the following page. Mix them up and spread them out on a table facedown. Play the game with two or three other people. Take turns turning over two cards at a time, trying to match each situation with the card that describes it. When a match is made, player collects those two cards. The winner is the person with the most cards at the end of the game.

The younger son wanted his inheritance.	The son tried to duck his dad's authority by moving out of town.	The kind of activities the son pursued in the foreign land.
The great kind of friends that the son picked up.	How his friends helped him invest his money.	Where the son's inheritance went.
How many of the young man's friends came forward to help him out.	The chateau the young man lived in after his bucks ran out.	The young man's roommates after his "friends" left him.
His cuisine that accompanied the job he finally found.	What finally happened to his brain when he hit bottom.	What happened in the land he moved to.
Where he headed when things got bad enough.	What he probably feared might happen to him if he showed his face around home again.	What his dad did when he saw him.

The Lost Son Game,
(continued)

HOW 'BOUT A RAISE?

What would you get as a response if you asked your parents:

(Match the question with the probable response.)

1. How 'bout a raise in my allowance?

2. How 'bout making my sister do all my chores?

3. How 'bout just letting me do what I want since I didn't ask to be born?

4. How 'bout gettin' me a motorcycle for my birthday?

5. How 'bout not making me go to school today?

GIVE US THIS DAY OUR DAILY BREAD:

A glimpse into the strange and wonderful world of George Müller.

In 1835 a young immigrant from Germany decided that God wanted him to improve the appalling conditions of inner city Bristol, England. All around him Müller saw children living out of crates and boxes, sharing the remains of garbage heaps with rats. Children of seven years of age were forced to work twelve-hour days in factories for a few pennies. Most were beaten mercilessly if they complained. Abuse of every kind abounded. Those who escaped the factories were forced to live on the streets by their wits.

Since most of these children were orphans or had been abandoned by their parents, there was seldom a caring adult in their lives. George Müller decided to change the situation. He would start an orphanage. (Government-run care homes were not in existence at this time.)

But George Müller had a problem; he had no money—not one penny. And lots of money would be needed to rent a building, buy food, clothing and bedding. But this did not discourage George. He knew someone who had wealth beyond measure. He would simply ask Him for some help.

So George prayed. In his diary he recorded that falling on his knees he asked God for one thousand pounds (English money) to pay for a building and for suitable people to care for the children. As he read the Bible his eyes fell upon the verse, “Open wide your mouth and I will fill it” (Ps. 81:10).

Four days later, unasked-for provisions began to appear at George Müller’s home. Although Müller had shared his idea with few people, God now began to work, motivating people to give money for the orphanage that had been just an idea in George Müller’s mind.

Within several months there was an orphan house in Bristol. Within a year there were three—each one of them paid for by money that was never asked for publicly, but prayed for privately by George Müller and his staff. There were no “Live Aid” programs or TV shows featuring starving children, yet the money came for the food and provisions, often at the last moment.

Time after time, Müller’s workers would find the provision cupboard only capable of handling one more meal. The staff would quietly gather and pray. And by the next mealtime there would be food left on the front porch or money slipped into the mail slot from someone who was “moved” by God to donate to this work.

Never asking for even a coin or telling his need to anyone but the Lord, George Müller and his staff fed, clothed and housed two thousand orphans from the streets of Bristol. They raised millions of dollars to pay for this mission, much of it not coming until the very instant it was needed.

Müller’s concept was that God could and would keep His promises and supply the daily bread of His children. As Müller worked and prayed, God did just that.

NO COMMENT

The guy who did these comics forgot to add the dialogue explaining what was going on. Please look up the verses and write the dialogue for him. Then match the captions on the next page with the correct cartoons. (Write the letter of each statement in the circle next to the cartoon it matches.)

NO COMMENT, continued

A God wants us to humbly ask Him for things we need, not greedily ask Him for things we want.

B We don't need to worry about getting what we need because we can trust God to take care of us.

C God wants us to concentrate on Him instead of concentrating on our needs.

D Jesus cares about our everyday needs.

E God uses us to meet each other's needs.

Make Your Own Request

Using the words below each line (or choosing your own words) create a prayer that suggests how you really think and feel about our giving God.

Prayer Blocker

Something is blocking Leroy's prayers from getting any farther than the ceiling.
Put together the letters to see what it is!

N___ ______V___ ___E___

T	R	O	I	T
R	S	F	N	O
O	G	G	I	H

The Hoarder of Hurts

THERE ONCE WAS A HOARDER OF HURT
WHO COLLECTED GOSSIP AND DIRT
AND BROUGHT IT INSIDE
TO KEEP IT ALIVE
AND WITH IT HE OFTEN WOULD FLIRT.

IF EVER A BARB CAME HIS WAY
OR A JEST ON HIM SOMEONE WOULD PLAY
HE'D COLLECT THEM ALL UP
WITH A SNEER AND HARRUMP
SO THE HURT WOULD GET LARGER EACH DAY.

ONE DAY THE HOARDER WENT IN
TO CHECK ON THE HURT CAUSED TO HIM,
BUT THE HURTS MULTIPLIED
AND ATE HIM ALIVE
AND HE WAS NEVER HEARD OF AGAIN.

1. What do you think this limerick is talking about?
2. What kind of person is the Hoarder of Hurts?
3. What danger is there in being this kind of person?

Forgive-O-Meter

In the graph below, chart which hurts and wrongs would be hard for you to forgive and which would be easy.

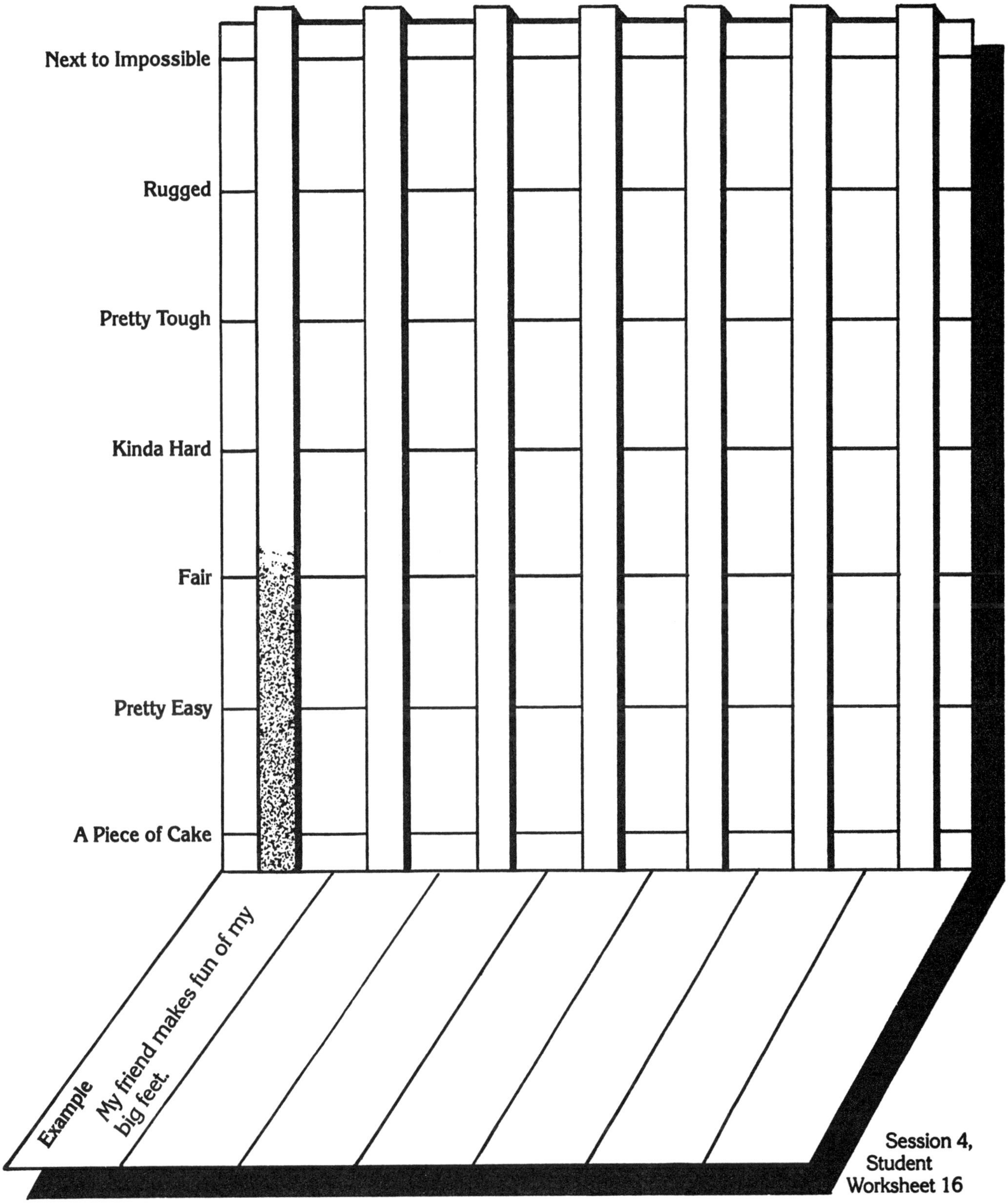

Session 4, Student Worksheet 16

START
PICK A CARD
PICK A CARD
GOSSIP!
GOSSIP!
ROLL AGAIN
PICK A CARD
LOSE A TURN
PICK A CARD
HEE HEE
HARDY-HAR!
TIME TO CLEAN UP YOUR ROOM!
PICK A CARD
PICK A CARD
ROLL AGAIN
PICK A CARD
ROLL AGAIN
SEX -R- US
PICK A CARD
THE REASON I WAS LATE? UH... WELL...
BREW
BARFO BEER
PICK A CARD
"YOU'VE GOT THE BIGGEST EARS I'VE EVER SEEN, DUMBO!"
PICK A CARD
ROLL AGAIN
LOSE A TURN
ROLL AGAIN
SIZZLE!
PICK A CARD
PICK A CARD
SUPER X RATED
VCR
CANDY
Yummy
PICK A CARD
PICK A CARD
ROLL AGAIN

Will you give in to temptation or become strong in the Lord? Find out in the

STICKY SITUATION GAME!

Instructions: Form groups of four. Use coins or other small objects for markers. Players place markers on start and throw number cube to determine the number of spaces to be moved.
The object of the game is to reach the "Strong in the Lord" side of the game board. Players follow directions on spaces where indicated. Whenever a player lands on space marked "Pick a card," he or she draws a Sticky Situation card and reads it aloud. Then player rolls the number cube again. If an odd number is rolled the player reads the unwise choice marked "odd" and moves three squares back. If an even number is rolled, player reads the wise choice marked "even" and remains on the same space. Whoever reaches the "Strong in the Lord" space first is the winner.

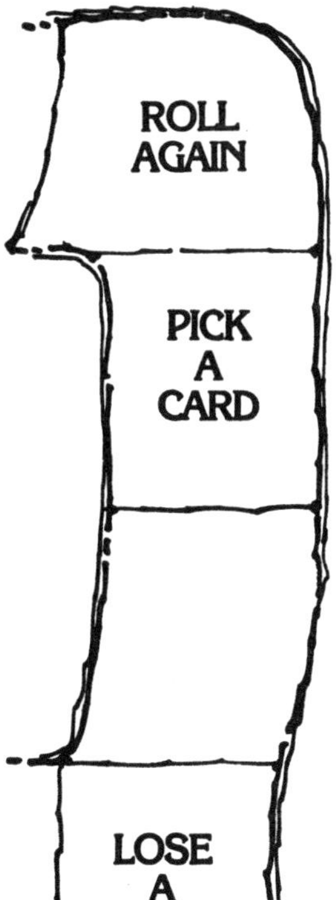

Sticky Situation Cards

You got home late and when your mom asked why, you lied. Later you feel guilty.

(odd) You convince yourself one little lie won't hurt anything.

(even) You ask God's forgiveness and tell your mom the truth.

You get home from school to find your little sister has totally messed up your room.

(odd) You scream at her, tell your mom, and pout.

(even) You pray for God's help to be calm before you talk to your sister.

You and your friend are at a Youth Group meeting. Your friend wants to whisper and laugh during the Bible study.

(odd) You never pass up a chance for a good laugh.

(even) You listen to the leader which lets your friend know what is important to you right now.

On Saturday morning you wake up early with nothing to do.

(odd) You watch cartoon reruns on TV.

(even) You read your Bible, or ask your mom if there's anything she'd like you to do for her.

Your older brother rented a video that shows a lot of graphic violence and sex. You know you shouldn't watch it.

(odd) You keep walking by the room where your brother is watching it.

(even) You call a friend and go to the park.

At night when you are falling asleep you remember how a kid at school made fun of you.

(odd) You think of all the mean things you could do to get back at him.

(even) You try to understand why this person acted that way and pray for him.

Some friends ask you to come over. You think they plan to look at dirty magazines.

(odd) You go to see what they will do.

(even) You make other plans for the day.

A friend comes up and says, "Wait till you hear what Tony told Sherri about John and Tammy!"

(odd) You pull your friend into a corner and whisper, "What?"

(even) You say, "Let's talk about something else."

Your friends invite you to a party where kids will be drinking beer and smoking marijuana. If you go, you might want to join in.

(odd) You go anyway and plan to leave early if things get rough.

(even) You invite some other friends over to listen to Christian music.

Your mom yells from the other room that you need to clean your room.

(odd) You act like you didn't hear her.

(even) You remember that pleasing our parents pleases the Lord and you get to work.

A great movie is on TV but you know you need to study for a test. If you don't study you'll be tempted to cheat in class.

(odd) You watch the movie and study during the commercials, sort of.

(even) You study for the test until you feel ready to do well.

At lunch the group you are eating with starts making fun of a girl who dresses differently from everyone else. You are tempted to join in.

(odd) You laugh too.

(even) You say something nice about the girl.

Your sister has a candy stash on her dresser and you are hungry.

(odd) You go stand in front of the dresser, look at the candy and try to decide if you should take some.

(even) You go make yourself a sandwich.

It's time to pray at Sunday School. Group members are invited to offer sentence prayers.

(odd) You let your mind wander and almost fall asleep.

(even) Even though it's scary, you pray out loud and feel closer to God.

WHAT'S THE DIFF?

Lydia

Hi! My name is Lydia. I live in an apartment with my mom and three sisters. Sometimes my sisters really get on my nerves! My youngest one is always wanting to be with me and my friends. She won't leave me alone. Yesterday I really yelled at her. Later I felt bad though. I told her I was sorry. I asked God to forgive me too. Sometimes I like to find a quiet place in the house and be all alone. I read my Bible and talk to God about my problems.

On Tuesday nights I go to the youth group at my church. I like the Bible studies and being with Christian friends. At school a lot of the kids don't believe in God like I do. Like Sheila—cheating on a test is nothing to her. She wanted me to cheat with her. I try not to do what Sheila does, but I can still be her friend.

Mark

I'm Mark. I live in a house with my mom and dad and older sister. My mom and dad make me go to Sunday School but I don't like it. My friend and I write notes during the Bible study and laugh at the Christian kids.

What I really like is riding my skateboard and hanging around with my friends. Ray is one of my friends. He is really cool. He is always making us crack up by telling dirty jokes. Once he took me to a party where kids were smoking marijuana. I didn't really want to try it but I didn't want Ray to laugh at me, so I did. My parents would kill me if they knew. I know they want me to obey God, but that seems impossible to me. I wish I had someone to talk to about my problems.

Read each verse. Write down what Lydia did to help her resist temptation. Then write down what Mark did that made it hard for him to resist temptation.

__________________________ **Psalm 119:9,10** __________________________

__________________________ **Proverbs 1:10** __________________________

__________________________ **Philippians 4:13** __________________________

__________________________ **1 Thessalonians 5:17** __________________________

__________________________ **1 John 1:9** __________________________

TANGLED UP?

All of us face temptations every day but God can help us to not give in. Locate the sentence that best describes the way you feel.

GUESS my CELEBRITY

THE MAGAZINE THAT TELLS ALL!

Write at least five clues which describe a famous person—someone who is probably known to everyone in your group.

1.

2.

3.

4.

5.

6.

7.

NEWS

After you have written your clues, you will be asked to read them to your group. Keep track of how many clues you have to read before they guess correctly.

$2.00

CLOSE ENCOUNTERS WITH GOD

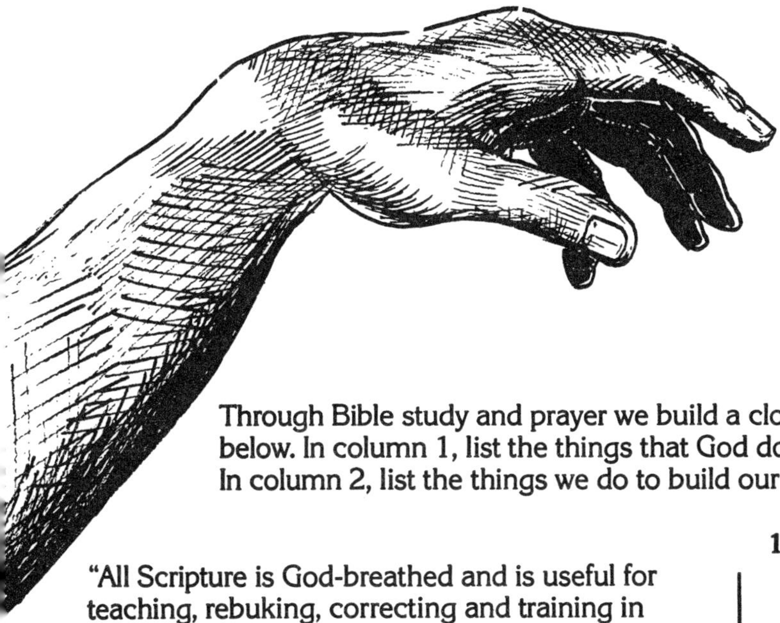

Through Bible study and prayer we build a close relationship with God. Read each verse below. In column 1, list the things that God does to build His relationship with us. In column 2, list the things we do to build our relationship with God.

	1. Things God does.	2. Things we do.
"All Scripture is God-breathed and is useful for teaching, rebuking, correcting and training in righteousness, so that the man of God may be thoroughly equipped for every good work." 2 Timothy 3:16,17		
"I meditate on your precepts and consider your ways. I delight in your decrees; I will not neglect your word." Psalm 119:15,16		
"The unfolding of your words gives light; it gives understanding to the simple." Psalm 119:130		
"The Lord is near to all who call on him, to all who call on him in truth." Psalm 145:18		
"Show me your ways, O Lord, teach me your paths; guide me in your truth and teach me, for you are God my Savior, and my hope is in you all day long." Psalm 25:4,5		
"I call on the Lord in my distress, and he answers me." Psalm 120:1		

Cut along dotted lines. Place pages and cover together and staple them to form a "Together Time Journal." Each day this week read some verses of Scripture and let God speak to you. Then talk with God. Write your thoughts in this journal.

TOGETHER TIME JOURNAL

1 Look up Psalm 119:9-16 and read it:
What God said to me through His Word:

What I talked to God about:

2 Look up Proverbs 2:1-5 and read it:
What God said to me through His Word:

What I talked to God about:

3 Look up Matt. 25:14-30 and read it:
What God said to me through His Word:

What I talked to God about:

4 Look up Hebrews 4:12-13 and read it:
What God said to me through His Word:

What I talked to God about:

5 Look up Luke 18:18-30 and read it:
What God said to me through His Word:

What I talked to God about:

6 Look up Isaiah 55:8-9 and read it:
What God said to me through His Word:

What I talked to God about:

7 Look up Psalm 119:97-104 and read it:
What God said to me through His Word:

What I talked to God about:

YOU CAN COUNT ON IT

When God says He will do something, you can count on it because He is faithful. Read each verse about God's faithfulness. Then match each verse and its message to a situation below by filling in the blanks.

"He hears the prayers of the righteous." Proverbs 15:29

"For I am convinced that neither death nor life, neither angels nor demons, neither the present nor the future, nor any powers, neither height nor depth, nor anything else in all creation, will be able to separate us from the love of God that is in Christ Jesus our Lord." Romans 8:38,39

"And this is what he promised us—even eternal life." 1 John 2:25

"He will keep you strong to the end, so that you will be blameless on the day of our Lord Jesus Christ." 1 Corinthians 1:8

"And my God will meet all your needs according to his glorious riches in Christ Jesus." Philippians 4:19

"If we confess our sins, he is faithful and just and will forgive us our sins and purify us from all unrighteousness." 1 John 1:9

____________ teaches that God will be faithful to ____________ us.

____________ teaches that God will help us be ____________.

____________ teaches that God will faithfully ____________.

____________ says that God can be counted on to give us ____________.

____________ says that nothing can ____________ us from ____________.

____________ says God will ____________ the ____________ of the righteous.

Grateful Graffiti

Fill in the blanks below to tell reasons you are grateful for God's faithfulness in your life.

Thanks God, for...

meeting my needs by

hearing me when I prayed for

giving me strength when

forgiving me when I

protecting me by

What Do You Expect?

Judgment Day is the time when all of mankind will stand before God. He will tell each of us what He thinks of our lives and what our future will be. Circle the cartoon that best describes how you picture God on Judgment Day, or draw your own idea at the bottom of the page.

More for Your Money

Narrator: There once was a man by the name of Gus
Who owned a store called "Pets Is Us."
Gus was planning to go out of town,
So he called his workers and gave the lowdown.

Gus: I'm going away, but I want this understood:
Take what I give you and do something good!
Have I made myself perfectly clear?
Repeat it back so I can hear.

3 Workers: You're going away, but you want this understood:
"Take what I give you and do something good!"

Gus: I'll give you money in amounts high or low,
Use whatever I give to make business grow.

3 Workers: We love our pets. We love our boss, Gus.
We'll do our best for "Pets Is Us".

Narrator: To a real good worker by the name of Nash,
Gus gave a giant box full of cash.
To a worker who went by the name of Sonny,
Gus gave a purse containing lots of money.
To the last worker, whose name was Hank,
He gave his daughter's piggy bank.

Gus: Whether you have a little or a lot,
Just do your best with what you've got.
Just do your best is all I ask,
I'll see you all when I get back.

Narrator: So Gus left town with his wife and his kid.
Now let's find out what the workers did.

Nash: Wow, the boss gave me a box of cash.
I think I'll use it to clean up trash.
If it's a lot cleaner in our store,
More customers will come through the door.
I'll use some money to buy a bus,
To bring more people to "Pets Is Us".
The bus will bring them here, we'll spread the word.
They'll come buy a pet—dog, cat or bird.

Sonny: Well, I didn't get as much cash as Nash,
But with what I **did** get, I'll throw a bash.
I'll give our pets a fun-filled party,
I'll make sure they all eat hearty.
Then just watch, I'd be willing to bet,
More people will buy our happy pets.

Hank: Nash and Sonny! Cash and Money!
My situation is not funny!
I got such a small amount!
I'm not even going to count!
I can't stand that so and so.
We have to work so **his** store can grow!
I'll show him. A hole I'll dig!
I'll throw in my coins, with this little pig!

Narrator: After awhile, when his trip was through,
Gus came to the store and called his crew.

Gus: When I came back to "Pets Is Us",
New customers were getting off a bus.
They were shopping in a nice, clean store,
Nash—good job, I'll give you more!

Nash: You'll give me more! Oh, this is great!
Working for you is really first rate!

Gus: I see all the pets are looking hearty,
I heard you gave them a little party.
That was a super idea, Sonny!
Next time I'll give you more money!

Sonny: Thank you, Gus, though I'm just a clerk
You always notice how hard I work.

Gus: Now can we talk, my friend Hank?
What did you do with your little bank?

Hank: You'll find the bank in a hole in the ground!

Gus: Hank, you are lazy. You just sat around.
With what I gave you, you didn't even try.
You're fired, that's it, so long, bye-bye!

Here Comes the Judge

Check the boxes that best describe how you feel:

☐ I'm not concerned about Judgment Day.

☐ I know I'm not ready for Judgment Day.

☐ I've never taken Jesus seriously.

☐ I realize now that I need to get ready for Judgment Day.

☐ I would like to accept Jesus as my Savior and dedicate my life to Him.

☐ I've given my life to Jesus but I know I need to do more with what He's given me.

☐ I am confident that I'm in God's family and I'm doing my best for Him. I'll continue to look for ways to know and serve Him each day.

☐ I need more information. How can I accept Jesus as my Savior?

☐ ____

Think about the statement(s) you checked. Now what should you do about your statement? Write your plan below. (Examples: I will talk to my teacher about becoming a Christian, or I will read my Bible on my own every night.)

My Plan of Action is . . .

What's the Word?

Your job is to find the word we are looking for. Do this by using your pencil to draw a route from Start to Finish on the maze, collecting letters along the way. When you have finished, unscramble the letters to try and form the word we want. The trouble is, there is more than one path from Start to Finish! It might be hard to figure out which path is the right one and which letters are the right ones, so we'll give you two hints: The correct path is the shortest one and the word is seven letters long.

Stiff Competition?

If you take a look at the game below, you'll notice it contains several things that can become more important to us than God—like the wealth that tripped up the rich ruler. There are also some blanks for you and your partner to fill in with things you've thought of. (Hint: Think of things that are temptations people like you face—temptations are things that compete with God.)

When you have filled in as many blanks as you can, use your pencil to trace a path along the wires from the Start to the Finish. Along the way, go through as few boxes as you can. (Blank boxes count double.) The people who create the path with the least things that compete with God are the winners—of the game, and in real life!

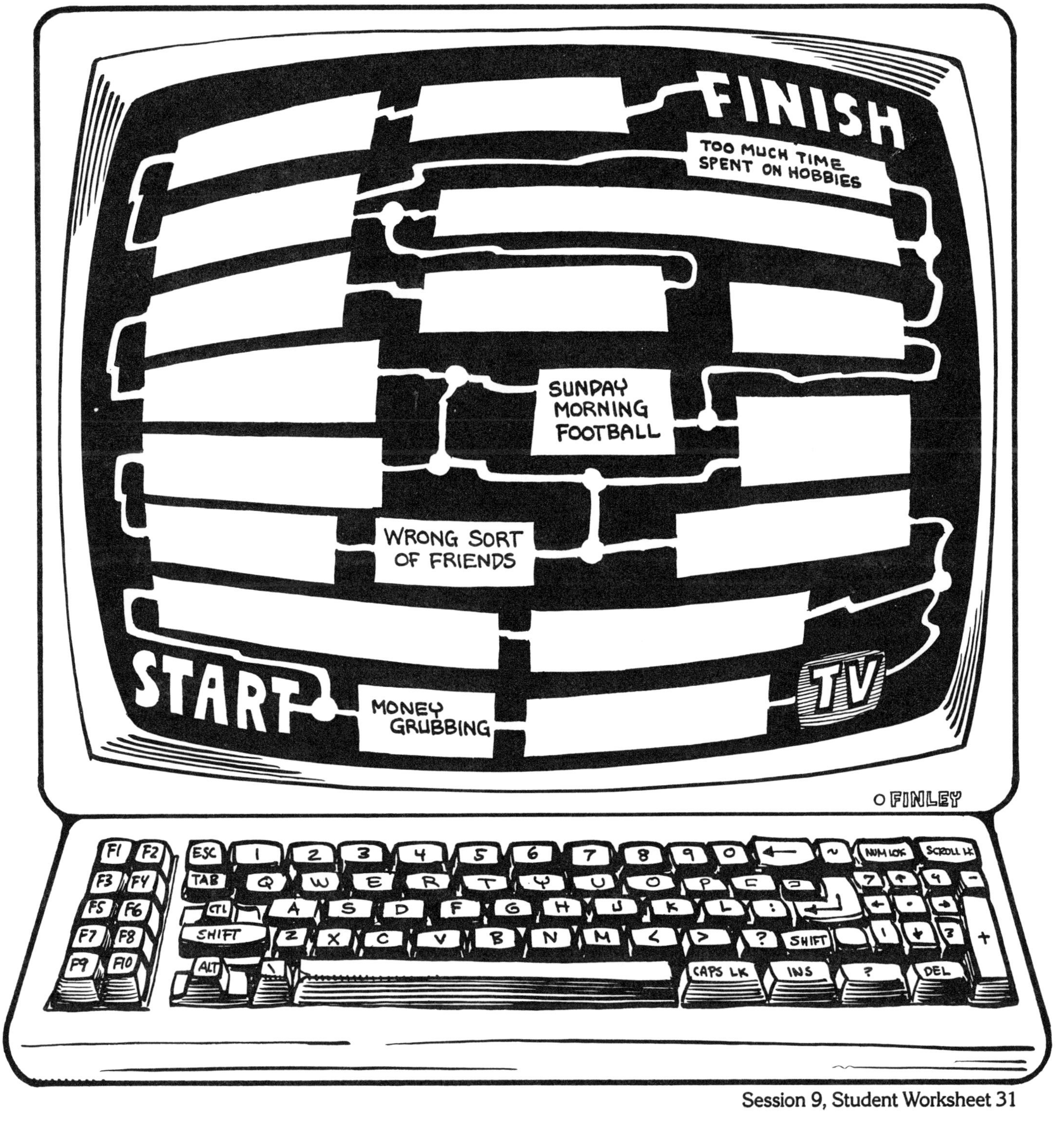

Reason to Be Jealous

1. God is the most important thing to me

   ☐ all the time
   ☐ most of the time
   ☐ hardly ever
   ☐ never

2. I find myself giving up things in order to spend time with God

   ☐ often
   ☐ sometimes
   ☐ once in a while
   ☐ never

3. If God were jealous of anything in my life it might be ______________________________

   ____

4. Now that I know God is a jealous God I would like to ______________________________

   ____

   ____

From This Angle

One day five blind men went to the zoo. Here's what happened . . .

Create your own blind man dilemma below.

★ BEYOND DESCRIPTION ★

There is no question that God is far greater than we can possibly imagine, but in what ways? Discover for yourselves as you complete the crossword puzzle below.

Across:

1. We can never ______ everything about God.
3. To find someone greater than God would be ______.
10. A word that means "unable to be fully understood."
11. Where God is.
12. This word means "goes on forever."
17. God's judgments are ______. (Romans 11:33.)
18. We look at a person's appearance, but God looks at the ______. (1 Samuel 16:7.)
20. God is so big that people are like ______ to him. (Isaiah 40:22.)
21. Isaiah 44:6 says, God is first and ______. (See 4 down.)
22. According to Isaiah 55:8,9 you can never hope to ______ like God.
23. God is so big that nations are like ______ on a scale (see 15 down). (Isaiah 40:15.)
24. In the beginning, God created ______ and earth. (Genesis 1:1.)

Down:

2. This word means "lasting forever."
4. There is only ______ God.
5. Another name for "Maker."
6. Jeremiah 23:24 says, "Do I not ______ heaven and earth?" (See 16 down.)
7. There is so much to know about God. Learning about Him should never be ______.
8. We can always ______ more about God.
9. Compared to God's strength we are ______.
13. God is ______ and last. (See 21 across.)
14. God is far ______ human understanding.
15. Isaiah 49:15 says that God is so big that nations are like a ______ in a bucket.
16. Jeremiah 23:34 says, "Do I not fill heaven and ______?" (See 6 down.)
19. No one is ______ to God. (Isaiah 49:25.)

Design-It-Yourself Section!

The following pages contain all sorts of fun artwork. Use them for mail outs, bulletins, and overhead projector transparencies. Cut 'em out, paste 'em up, and there you have it!

Special note: To help you design your own materials, two very popular books are available—**The Youth Worker's Clip Art Book** and its sequel, **The Youth Worker's Son of Clip Art Book!** For information, please see back cover.

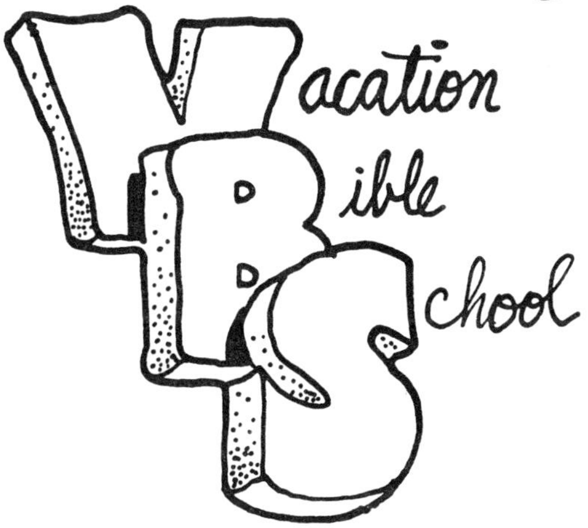

COMING☆UP...

COMING☆UP...

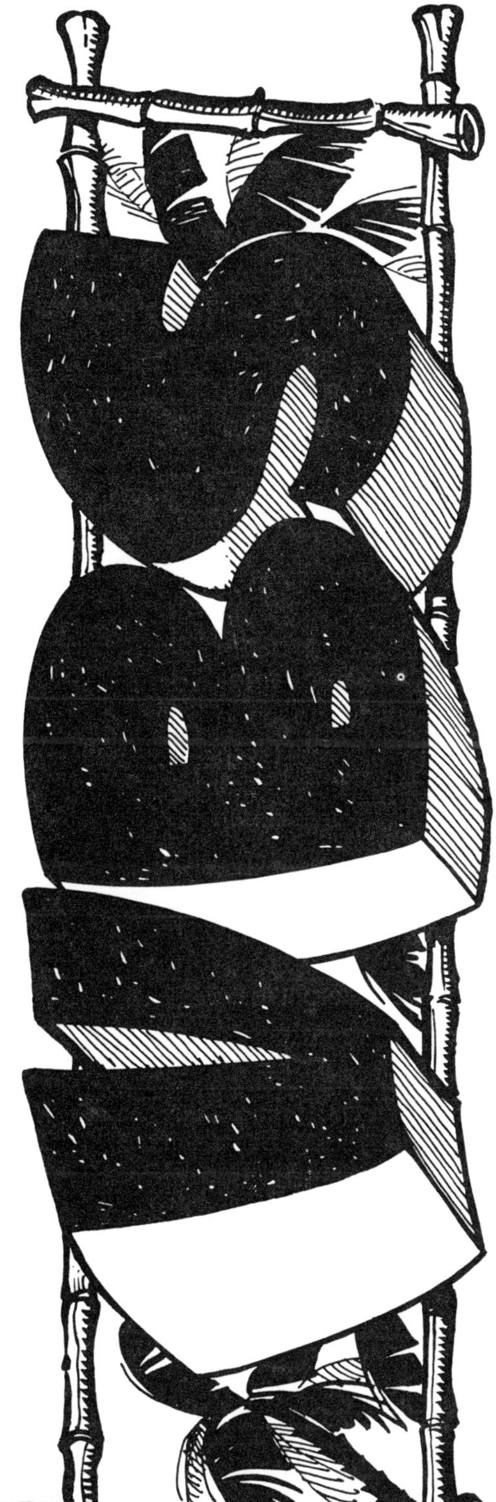

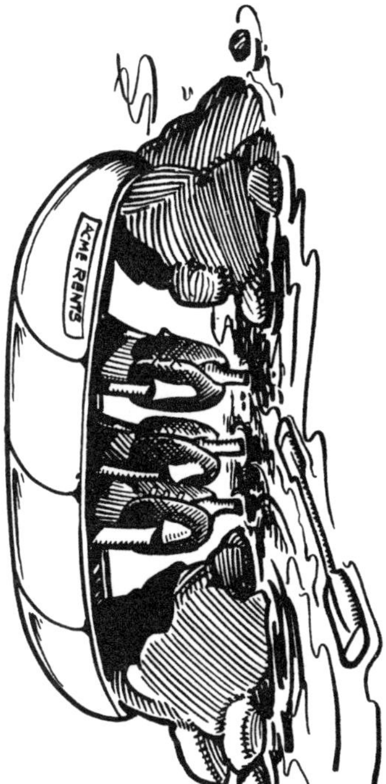

A SUMMER YOU'LL NEVER FORGET!
JOIN US!
FEARLESS LEADER
MIDDLE school
SUMMER

FEARLESS LEADER

MIDDLE school

SUMMER